Jimmy Dorrell is one of the best pastors on the planet. His ragamuffin congregation at Church Under the Bridge is one of the clearest glimpses of the Kingdom I've ever seen. For decades, Jimmy has been studying like a scholar and getting his hands dirty like a saint. He loves the Church, and because of that love, he is not willing to accept Her as She is. May this book move us all a little closer to the Church we dream of.

Shane Claiborne
Author, activist, recovering sinner . . . and one of the
compilers of *Common Prayer*, a resource to unite
people in prayer and action

Many Christ-followers today are disillusioned, disconnected, and disappointed with the current expressions of church. Jimmy Dorrell puts forth a compelling case that although the world is changing around us at breakneck speed, the church is often an unchanging island to itself, and it is only the churches that can adaptively change that will be the ones that thrive in every generation. Just because "Jesus Christ is the same yesterday and today and forever" does not mean that the expression of his church should be static. This is not a book of quick fixes but a primer for bringing about the deep change that reflects the selfless heart of the gospel in every generation. Jimmy is not a peddler of doom but a prophet of hope for what the church can be today.

Eric Swanson
Missional Specialist, Leadership Network
Co-author of *To Transform a City* and *The*
Externally Focused Quest

Dead Church Walking

DEAD CHURCH WALKING

Giving Life to the Church That Is Dying to Survive

JIMMY DORRELL

Biblica Books
from InterVarsity Press

InterVarsity Press
P.O. Box 1400, Downers Grove, IL 60515-1426
World Wide Web: www.ivpress.com
Email: email@ivpress.com

© 2011 by Jimmy Dorrell

InterVarsity Press® is the book-publishing division of InterVarsity Christian Fellowship/ USA®, a movement of students and faculty active on campus at hundreds of universities, colleges and schools of nursing in the United States of America, and a member movement of the International Fellowship of Evangelical Students. For information about local and regional activities, write Public Relations Dept., InterVarsity Christian Fellowship/USA, 6400 Schroeder Rd., P.O. Box 7895, Madison, WI 53707-7895, or visit the IVCF website at www.intervarsity.org.

All Scripture quotations taken from the HOLY BIBLE, NEW INTERNATIONAL VERSION® NIV® Copyright © 1973, 1978, 1984, 2011 by Biblica, Inc.™. Used by permission of Biblica, Inc.™. All rights reserved worldwide.

Originally published by Biblica.

ISBN 978-0-8308-5632-9

Printed in the United States of America ∞

 InterVarsity Press is committed to protecting the environment and to the responsible use of natural resources. As a member of Green Press Initiative we use recycled paper whenever possible. To learn more about the Green Press Initiative, visit www.greenpressinitiative.org.

Library of Congress Cataloging-in-Publication Data is available through the Library of Congress.

P	17	16	15	14	13	12	11	10	9	8	7	6	5	4	3	2	1
Y	27	26	25	24	23	22	21	20	19	18	17	16	15	14	13		

Contents

PREFACE

PREFACE

Anyone who is to find Christ must first find
the church. How could anyone know where
Christ is and what faith is in him unless he
knew where his believers are?
—Martin Luther

Churches all over our nation are dying. Each week, thousands of Christians walk away from churches and hundreds of church buildings are shuttered, while others cling to life. "Every year more than 4000 churches close their doors compared to just over 1000 new church starts . . . Every year 2.7 million church members fall into inactivity" (Dr. Richard J. Krejcir, Schaeffer Institute, http://www.truespirituality.org). At the same time, some church-planting networks proclaim that new church starts outnumber closures. It's a tumultuous time for the bride of Christ. While it may be tempting to ignore these shifts, the future of the church is too important for us to look away. After all, Christ died for the church. If it meant that much to God, how can we ignore what is happening—and what might happen soon—to the church?

An avalanche of books, articles, sermons, and lectures about change have buried the average church. Many of these well-intended efforts seem to have a "blame the victim" mindset that only discourages the discouraged. No church can simply wake up one day and be completely different, especially after years or centuries of entrenchment and tradition. It's like blaming an addict for not changing on their own. A congregation that recognizes the *need* for change may not be sure *how* to change, or even *what* to change into!

This book is about both the process and the goal of change. How does a congregation determine what it wants to be? How do churched people understand a growing nonchurch culture? What should change, and what can stay the same? What is the cost of transformation? Any congregation that chooses to change for the sake of God's kingdom can expect challenges and opportunities for growth in equal measure.

Change isn't easy. In fact, it's probably the most painful process a church can undergo. But the towering waves of uncertainty and fear don't have to drown us—they may simply be an opportunity for Jesus to stand at the helm of our church and shout, "Quiet! Be still!" as he rebukes the wind and calls us to faith. (See also Matthew 8:26 and James 1:6.)

Is your church dying? Take a deep breath, and take hope: the Giver of Life has designed you for change. There is life ahead.

INTRODUCTION

INTRODUCTION
CONSIDERING CHANGE

Churches simply cannot make significant changes and keep all of their people pleased. Not everyone is pleased now.
—Michael Emerson and Christian Smith

Change Happens

Sometimes change happens *to* us, and sometimes we cause it, but either way we have to deal with it.

Many of us are reluctant to choose change, especially if we are in traditional churches that have experienced past days of growth and glory. But even though we can't control whether change comes, "we can choose whether to embrace or resist it. We can choose the kind of changes that advances the kingdom of God into our world, or we can retreat into a subculture that attempts to isolate us from the world" (Stetzer and Rainer, *Transformational Church*, 2–3).

Even while our world and country and neighborhoods change, often in a positive direction, thousands of church buildings and congregations continue to fall apart and fail. Pastors and key leaders have moved on to more exciting opportunities, leaving dying churches behind. Yet many of those who remain still long for more, aware of the impending funeral of their church in a few years if something does not happen soon. They are ready to face the challenges of changing churches in a postmodern and increasingly post-Christian nation.

There are no easy formulas or quick fixes. Real, lasting change is difficult and often painful. There are no guarantees that the process will lead to a renewed or missional church. Yet the journey and effort themselves bring new life to those who are willing to walk toward the kingdom of God. And the alternative is to stay where we are as churches and face our inevitable death.

Rose-Colored Glasses in a Blizzard

We humans have an uncanny ability to ignore, distort, and flee reality. It's hard to see ourselves as we really are. Our lenses are colored by our own experiences, our context, and our hopes—so much so that it's hard to be sure what we're really seeing. Paradoxically, we are often ready to defend the status quo in our own lives and in organizations we care deeply about, while at the same time being quick to point out the hypocrisy of others. Consider the following situations that would make us want to scream, *"How can you be so out of touch with reality?!"*

- At a hospital you see a patient, strapped to his oxygen bottle, standing outside the oncology ward and smoking a pack of cigarettes.
- At an all-you-can-eat buffet you sit near an obese woman in a wheelchair who is polishing off a second slice of cake after three trips to the food bar.

- At the mall you witness the police arresting the teenage daughter of a wealthy friend for shoplifting clothes, and you know she has access to more money than you do.

Yet as troubling as these images are, when we're honest with ourselves we know that we can be just as self-destructive and hypocritical—and so can the organizations we care about, like our churches. In fact, some of the very things we cherish the most may be part of the problem, like the cigarettes the cancer patient continues clutching.

If we are to change graciously and effectively as people and churches—and remember, we *are* going to change—we must begin by striving to see ourselves and our churches as honestly as possible. We humans are God's highest creation, made in his image and for his glory, and the church is the body of Christ in the world. That's why God lovingly calls us to change—because he wants his people and his church to look more and more like him.

As we change, Christians have the advantage of the Spirit's power, and we have been given the incredible freedom to openly confess our own condition and thereby begin to change it. Scripture calls this *transformation*, and the good news is that it is available to every man, woman, and child—and church!—who chooses to enter the process in the power of the Spirit.

Is It Worth It?

The truth is that most of us would rather leave things the way they are than choose change. When talking about exercise and dieting, it's common to hear something like, "I'd rather die happy doing what I want than get on a treadmill and eat salads the rest of my life. Some things are better just left alone!" So it is with many churches. Asking probing questions, modifying hallowed traditions, and refocusing a congregation's vision can create myriad problems. Without a doubt, choosing to change has built-in cost and risk.

Many books have been written on "10 easy steps" and "untold secrets" of a successful ministry, but in reality there is no quick and painless process that will lead a church to change successfully. What works in one place fails miserably in another. The one trait found in all leaders of change is the willingness to risk. Pastor Larry Osborne says, "Highly successful leaders ignore conventional wisdom and take chances. What separates a successful risk taker from a bankrupt gambler? I've come to believe it's the ability to distinguish between a prudent risk and a wild-eyed gamble" (Shelley, *Empowering Your Church through Creativity and Change*, 151).

Since risk is so, well, *risky,* Osborne asks five basic questions that a congregation needs to answer in the process of change:

1. Who else has done it? (Asking others can minimize risks.)
2. How bad can it get? (What could go wrong? Is this the right time?)
3. Can I try it on for size? (A trial run can save a heartache.)
4. How much leverage do I have? (How much relational capital can I use?)
5. How clearly has God spoken? (Has the discernment been strong enough to move?)

These questions can give us hints and suggestions about what it might be like to finally take the risk and change—a process that has some common principles.

The Principles of Change

Change is a unique and complex process, filled with chaos, false expectations, prejudices, and futile efforts to control. Simplistic steps and checklists for implementing change mock the reality of its struggle. Since change is a dynamic process with a local context, what works well in one setting may be a disaster in another. However, there are eight basic principles of change that can help us think about the possibilities of successful transitions, and we'll look at one in each chapter.

1. **Change always includes choice** (chapter one: "Process"). True change cannot be forced on someone, and having only one choice is no choice at all. There are numerous ways to be and do church. Once the alternatives are seriously considered, the challenge of an agreed course of action follows. Church members need to come to some level of acceptance that guides the ongoing process and own the decision without coercion. A person cannot be forced to go on a diet or begin to exercise regularly. No matter how hard we try, we cannot make another person change. Love involves freedom, even if there is resistance or rejection. The unique members of each church must choose how to navigate the rough waters of change and transformation.

2. **Change is built on reality** (chapter two: "Presuppositions"). One of the hardest parts of the process of change is being willing to admit the facts, rather than clinging to what we *wish* was happening or what *used* to happen. If what is currently happening is not working, continuing the same course of action or behavior will be fruitless. Whether unmet budgets,

declining membership, or the reality of congregational
frustration and apathy, there comes a point when
significant numbers of members must openly admit
that the church is in trouble. While Band-Aid attempts
to address these issues may have been tried, the reality
is that fundamental changes need to be made. If a
majority of the congregation still believes that simply
improving the various components of church life will
turn the church around, it is likely not ready for the
challenges of genuine change.

3. **Change is built on purpose** (chapter three:
"Purpose"). Change must be undertaken for the
right reasons, especially if we are going to commit
significant time and energy to it. Since church
members have such wide expectations of why the
church exists and what it is supposed to do for them,
these discussions can be difficult and entangled. It
is critical that opinions are heard and noted, even if
they seem shallow and mundane. The list of temporal
ideas will likely rush to the forefront with statements
like, "We need a new pastor, a better building in a
new location, contemporary worship, and a dynamic
children's program that will reach new families."
Assurances that these various views will be considered
at the right time give members a sense of being heard.
Yet the leaders must help the congregation dig into
deeper issues such as the purpose of the church and
how to live out God's call in the local community. For
many church members, these are challenging thoughts
that may stretch them beyond their comfort levels.

4. **Change pushes the church into visible presence in the community** (chapter four: "Places"). Through the years, many congregations have cloistered themselves together in "come structures" of buildings and locations that rarely intersect with the unchurched world. In an era when church is no longer sought by outsiders, it is critical that the church engage in the local community in both word and deed. From worship in "third places" to acts of kindness and mercy among those in need, the church must become visible to the general public that sees it as marginalized and self-centered.

5. **Change requires trusted leadership** (chapter five: "Power"). Biblical trust is based on the faith that— *power* God will use his people and their gifts to form God-honoring churches. Many psychologists assert that the earliest stage of life, 0–18 months, is the critical time when trust or mistrust emerges, and later stages of development are built on this foundation. Since church transformation is a group process, the ability to trust one another is critical. "Without trust, there is no 'glue' to hold relationships together, and indeed no possibility" (Shoel, Prouty, and Radcliffe, *Islands of Healing*, 15). The role of leaders cannot be ignored. At some level, everyone is a leader, thus giving value to each member. Yet there are those who are naturally respected and acknowledged leaders who can create and sustain healthy dialogue and decision making.

6. **Change always includes risk** (chapter six: "Pain"). Change means journeying into the unknown and experiencing discomfort along the way. The temptation

to go back to the familiar system, even when if it was dysfunctional, constantly pulls at those in the process of change. Risk brings out our fears, and fear can immobilize us. "Obviously, fear is one of the most powerful emotions known to both animals and humans. Fears in people are primarily linked to threats to one's ego" (Ewert, *Outdoor Adventure Pursuits*, 71–72). Our self-esteem can be threatened by fear of rejection or failure. These are important challenges facing any church in the change process—and a recognition of the inevitable risk and pain required by change makes change all the more likely to be significant and lasting.

7. **Change requires constant renewal** (chapter seven: "Pitfalls"). Let's face it: frequent change can become wearisome and lead us back toward sinful patterns. Change takes energy, creativity, and time. And it's hard to continually find the internal resources to be positive and hopeful when we become depleted. Only if we regularly humble ourselves before God in our weakness can we find his strength. However, as frustrated church members grow tired of change, they are likely to become more divisive, give up, or experience emotional pitfalls—events that can be extremely damaging to the change process of the church.

8. **Change requires commitment** (chapter eight: "Possibilities"). Since change requires us to shift our opinions and habits, the process will undoubtedly become uncomfortable. If feelings dominate our choices more than the commitment to those we have been called to share life together with, there is

a likelihood that we will exit the process, physically
or emotionally, before lasting change happens.
Change means commitment over an extended time,
commitment to decisions that are made as a group,
and commitment to Christ as head of the church.
Many churches start the process of change only to
encounter discouraging breakdowns or incessant
delays. When church members become exasperated
and frustrated, it is easy to give up and look for
another church—or quit church altogether. Yet
commitment to one another in the family of God
under the lordship of Christ creates real freedom
and potential transformation. Even disagreements
become building blocks when relationships become
more important than ideas. God never gives up on his
church, and neither should we.

Orthodoxy Needs Orthopraxy for Real Change

What makes the process of church change so difficult is
that it has two inseparable parts—belief and action—that we
constantly try to separate. Many of us are willing to talk about
change, and even say that we need to change, but we struggle to
integrate believing in change with actually making changes.

This isn't a church problem; it's a modern, Western problem.
It's common to hear someone say, "Walk your talk," as if those
were two separate things. In the Hebraic worldview in the Old
Testament, to say something naturally meant doing it. To say
you loved God was to do his will. The relationship between word
and deed was so critical that the Levitical law outlined punish-
ment for discrepancies.

While to Hebrews doing the truth was foremost, to Greeks believing it was the key. This split is affecting us today. Many Christians claim a strong faith in God and see themselves as spiritual people, yet they act in ways that are in opposition to what they say they believe. Many have grown up in Christian homes and even attend church, but they seem to justify their inappropriate actions, even in light of biblical references that clearly see faith and action as integrated components of the whole truth. "In the same way, faith by itself, if it is not accompanied by action, is dead" (James 2:17).

This division of belief and action has caused many churches to swing to one of two extremes. Either churches have become so seeker friendly that they avoid topics on sin and repentance, or they have become rigid and judgmental against those who claim faith in Christ but live "worldly" lifestyles. Neither view is quite biblical, because belief and action are still separated.

Caught in the middle, one of the greatest challenges congregations face today is a diminished theology of church. Church has become optional for many who claim to be followers of Christ. Some would even say the church gets in the way of their faith. Formerly at the center of American life and all that was considered good, today the church is on the margins of society. While millions still attend each week, few seem to care what the church is doing and why—or if it's even doing anything at all. Yet based on a biblical view, the church is not optional, but a foundational pillar of the gospel. We were adopted into the family of God, called together to love God and love each other. This love cannot be mere words. Neither can this love be mere doctrine, used either to "attract" people to the good news or to "punish" people for their failures.

Around the country there are countless dying churches with solid doctrine. God never intended his church to believe the right things and yet be impotent in the culture. The apostle James's clarion call to the second generation of Christ followers was simple: "Do not merely listen to the word, and so deceive yourselves. Do what is says" (James 1:22). Real believing is doing. The two cannot be separated. To know God is to do his will. The challenge of change in the church has little to do with doctrine. Instead, it demands practical application of what we already know Jesus and the Scriptures are calling us to do. Anything less is not change at all.

Pilgrims' Progress

In the chapters ahead, we will discuss the signs of congregational anemia and offer solutions for health that can be life giving and redemptive. There is hope for the bride of Christ in our Western culture. Acknowledging that "we have a few problems" is not enough. The deeper question remains: What are you and your congregation willing to do to allow God to reshape you in his image? The journey may be difficult and sometimes painful. Real change always is. But even with all the challenges, the road to recovery and healing is the only one worth walking. The church remains God's symbol of hope pointing to a kingdom "on earth as it is in heaven." It is the same church that Jesus gave himself for, costing him everything. And in that same sacrificial spirit, we choose to walk down this road of becoming what he called us to be.

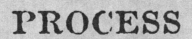

PROCESS

CHAPTER ONE
PROCESS

**The church is like Noah's ark: it stinks,
but if you get out, you'll drown.**

Checking Out on Checkups

The annual physical checkup can be an intimidating experience, which is why many Americans don't get one. The idea of being poked, prodded, and asked embarrassing questions by a doctor is an experience to which only hypochondriacs look forward.

It's more than the invasion of privacy that worries us, however—it's the expectation of change. What if our health provider pushes us to make changes we simply don't want to make? And what if we're told about an unanticipated illness or problem? Many of us live by the motto "If it ain't broke, don't fix it!" And even though our doctor can identify signs and symptoms of our impending "brokenness," many of us prefer to remain in blissful ignorance—at least until ignorance is no longer an option.

Change may be inevitable, but we generally prefer to avoid it as long as possible.

The receptionist at my doctor's office recently handed me a two-page inventory of personal questions to be completed before I could enter the exam room and wait some more. Had I ever had surgery, asthma, heart murmurs, acid reflux, dizziness, depression, hypertension, migraine headaches, swelling around the genitals, rashes, gout, an STD, arthritis . . . ? At each option, I wondered if my answer was sufficiently honest. I did have that *one* rash last spring. I do get depressed around certain holidays. And what's gout, anyway—maybe I had it without knowing!

The survey continued. Do I drink alcohol, coffee, or soft drinks? How much each day? Am I overweight? By how many pounds? Do I exercise? How often? Do I eat a lot of sweets or fatty foods? Are my parents alive? If not, what was their age at time of death and their cause of death? Have I ever signed a "do not resuscitate" form?

I was feeling healthy when I walked through the door, but the survey was enough to make me paranoid about everything in my body. Was my heart starting to murmur? Was that acid reflux I was tasting or just the burrito I ate for lunch? In just a few minutes, the nurse called my name and began the evaluation process that proved I was not long for this world. Then, after some casual chitchat, the doctor finalized my doom. He acted like it was no big deal, but his face told the real story.

He began to list everything that was wrong with me. "We need to do some blood work. We need to schedule you for a colonoscopy. I want to change your cholesterol medication." Then with deep seriousness he said, "You are going to have to make some lifestyle changes, or you will die soon!"

Wait—I'll *what?!*

All my senses were heightened to hear what came next. "You have some heart problems that must be addressed immediately. With your family history, extra weight, high-stress work, and lack of exercise, you're a walking time bomb. If you're going to live several more years, you must make changes in your diet, your work environment, and you must get serious about weight loss and exercise. There is nothing that will keep you from years more of good quality of life except your refusal to change."

Then he made sure my eyes were locked on his before he delivered his most important question: "Are you willing to make those changes?"

The walk to my car was a long one. I'd heard the words everyone dreads. My health was frail, my future was uncertain, and I couldn't keep living the same way or I would die. Unless I was willing to change, that is. Denial is how we usually deal with the need to change, even when the evidence is overwhelming that the problem is real and pressing. When we deny our problems, we are able to avoid thinking about how to change. But of course, avoiding change means that we can't start working to correct what is wrong. And in the case of my medical checkup, continued denial could have resulted in an untimely death.

When I processed what the doctor had told me, the conclusion was pretty simple: change or die.

The Church Must Change

The American church has just left the doctor's office, and the news isn't good. We have some heart problems that must be addressed immediately. With our family history, extra weight, high-stress work, and lack of exercise, we're a walking time bomb. There is nothing that will keep us from years more of quality life except our refusal to change, and we must get serious.

Are we willing to change?

A quick look at the European church should awaken North Americans, who often experience similar trends years later. While tourists still snap pictures of the breathtaking cathedrals, the pews are virtually deserted, abandoned by the "post-Christians" who gave up on the church and have embraced a pluralism that looks more like practical atheism. The Western church is in undeniable decline, even in North America. In the last few decades, the percentage of American Christians has dropped by more than 10 percent and is continuing to fall—and most people who have left the church have abandoned organized religion altogether.

While some American congregations are acknowledging the reality that our changing culture is no longer interested in church, many more congregations are choosing to live in denial. They've heard the bad news, but on the way out of the doctor's office they've already started thinking about something else. Some suggest that the decline of Christianity in Europe has little to do with the American church, while others blame bogeymen like liberalism and secularism while singing "Give Me That Old-Time Religion" even louder.

Yet make no mistake: the church in America *is* in trouble. Like me leaving the doctor's office with the bad news about my health, the choice is clear: change or die.

If you're already convinced of that, I'm going to try to galvanize you into action with a hard-hitting checklist of symptoms. And if you're still in denial about the sick state of the American church, I'm going to lay it all out for you in one place. In this case, ignorance isn't bliss.

"My guess is that out of one hundred churches, maybe ten would say they want transition. Most are happy as they are, or they'd rather die than change" (McLaren, *A New Kind of Christian*, 147). Even in the midst of obvious trends and "sister churches" going down, many church leaders prefer to ignore reality. Yet the realities are certainly cause for concern.

Eight Harsh Facts about the Western Church

- **Fact #1: The world changes even when the church doesn't.** From technology and demographics to consumer patterns and political opinions, American habits have altered. While most institutions, such as the marketplace and political campaigns, have adjusted to these changes the church often seems to be caught in a time warp, rudderless in the sea of change. A younger, more pluralistic generation considers itself to be "spiritual," but not "Christian," and growing numbers say church offers little that is worthy of time or attention. While large numbers of churches continue to operate just as they did half a century ago, other churches are struggling to understand and react to these rapid changes. "A growing number of people are leaving the institutional church for a new reason. They are not leaving because they have lost faith. They are leaving the church to preserve their faith. They contend that the church no longer contributes to their spiritual development" (McNeal, *The Present Future*, 4).

A slow decay into irrelevance isn't what Jesus wants from the church.

- **Fact #2: Churches and denominations in America are losing membership.** Even while a few researchers suggest that American religion is remarkably stable (Stark, *What Americans Really Believe*, 2), the religious landscape continues to change, and signs point to a decreasingly religious nation. The Pew Forum on Religion and Public Life suggests, "The U.S. religious marketplace is extremely volatile, with nearly half of American adults leaving the faith tradition of their upbringing to either switch allegiances or abandon religious affiliation altogether, a new study finds. While 78 percent is considered Christian in America, one in four adults ages 18–29 claim no affiliation with a religious institution." For Catholicism, the banner headline is that there are now 22 million ex-Catholics in America, by far the greatest net loss for any religious body" (John Allen, National Catholic Reporter, Feb. 11, 2011, http://ncrponline.org/). "Church membership declined in 2010 in over one-third of America's largest churches, including Southern Baptists, the nation's second largest denomination," according to the National Council of Churches 2011 Yearbook of American and Canadian Churches. "While mainstream Protestant denominations including the Lutherans (ELCA), Presbyterians (USA), and United Methodists have shown decreasing membership since 2007, non-denominational churches are gaining from the ranks of the unaffiliated" (Hartford Institute for Religion Studies: "Fast Facts about American Religion," http://hirr.hartsem.edu/research/fastfacts/fast_facts.html#sizecong). Many of those considered as cults by some Christians continued to increase in size. "Of the nation's 35 largest denominations, only four are growing," according to the yearbook. Two of those listed were the Mormons and Jehovah's Witnesses (http://hirr.hartsem.edu/ research/fastfacts/fast_facts.html#growlose). Though declining by 1.05 percent in 2010, many churches are maintaining, while those that had been declining in recent years continue to decline. Membership increased in the Assemblies of God and Pentecostals (Katherine T. Phan, *The Christian Post*, Feb. 15, 2011, http://www.christianpost.com/).

Demographic death is not where God is calling the church.

- **Fact #3: Church structures are costly.** Estimates of church building values run over $230 billion, severely strapping church budgets and missional opportunities. While new construction costs have inflated, most local churches struggle at the other end trying to maintain the seeming bottomless hole of repairs and utilities for old buildings. In the 2008–09 recession, church income on average fell 7–13 percent from previous years, yet the cost of utilities, insurance, and repairs increased. And more often, church members want their money designated for special activities or needs instead of the general budget, which pays for basic expenses. Yet a recent church building fund-raising campaign of a Dallas church raised $115 million for a new state-of-the-art downtown facility.

God never intended for *church* and *sanctuary* to be synonyms.

- **Fact #4: The unchurched continue to lose respect for Christian lifestyles.** The American church has compromised many of its core values, and people are noticing. "Perhaps the greatest obstacle to faithful witness on the part of Western Christianity is our failure to address the institutional compromises that we have made over the centuries" (Guder, *Continuing Conversion of the Church*, 204). While those outside the church frequently point out the inconsistency between the beliefs and actions of church members, church leaders caught in scandals continue to give credence to charges of hypocrisy. "According to a three-year study by the Barna Group, outsiders think Christians no longer represent what Jesus had in mind, that Christianity in our society is not what it was meant to be" (Kinnaman and Lyons, *Unchristian*, 15). Being judgmental and unloving have offended the non-Christians who do not want to be known for what they are against. For many outsiders, the church is primarily about being judgmental, especially about abortion and homosexuality. "Our judgments have boomeranged back on us—it was bound to happen, for we were explicitly warned by Jesus about this. The issue is our flagrant lack of mercy and compassion—the very things we so gratefully claim for ourselves" (Hirsch and Hirsch, *Untamed*, 222). According to several studies, the lifestyle of churchgoing Christians is generally no different from that of the non-Christian. "Among 20 lifestyle elements . . . the differences between the self-oriented behavior of born-again Christians and that of national norms was small. (Audrey Barrick, "Study Compares Christian and Non-Christian Lifestyles," *Christian Today*, February 7, 2007). "In American society, it is money and individual autonomy that are sacred, perhaps more sacred than even God, church, the gospel, and the Bible, for some American Christians" (Smith and Emerson, *Passing the Plate*, 194).

Authentic Christian living based on biblical convictions is critical in a culture growing ever more pluralistic.

- **Fact #5: The church is ineffective in the community.** If your church died, would the community be affected? Christians tend to see themselves as helpful and involved in their local communities, but surveys suggest they live virtually the same as their unchurched peers and are only minimally involved in the neighborhood. "Although born-again Christians are more likely to volunteer for their church, they are no more likely than average to help the poor or homeless" (Audrey Barrick, *Christian Today*, Feb. 7, 2007). From recycling to community development, the majority of Americans do very little to help their own cities. And while churches are increasingly touting involvement in social justice issues and restoring underresourced neighborhoods, churches still tend to see themselves as more effective in their overseas mission efforts than in their own communities. Efforts at racial reconciliation fare no better. In fact, according to some research, "white evangelicalism likely does more to perpetuate the racialized society than to reduce it" (Emerson and Smith, *Divided by Faith*, 170). From busy lifestyles to ungenerous giving, church members seem to be struggling to be effective wherever they live. Even community-based ministries struggle for financial support. While churches that contribute more to local ministries outside the church create more engaged followers, for most members security and comfort tend to be much more important than moral issues and community improvement. "American Christians . . . do not give money according to their objective financial capacity in income" (Smith and Emerson, *Passing the Plate*, 191). While there is a growing group of churches that are now engaging in Christian community development, the vast majority of churches are still disconnected from the neighborhoods in which they worship. If anything, they tend to simply offer benevolence and relieve needs through food pantries or clothes closets instead of involvement in more externally focused social action.

The church is God's body in the world—a body that is to be constituted of every tribe, tongue, and nation.

- **Fact #6: Pastoral leadership is declining.** According to numerous websites, between 1,500 and 1,800 pastors leave the ministry monthly, and 1,300 are terminated by the local church. The number one reason pastors leave the ministry is they discovered their church does not want to go the same direction as they feel led by God. Dealing with disgruntled church leaders and uncooperative members has had a huge impact on clergy decline. Closely behind is the long hours required, the negative impact of their job on their own family, moral failure, spiritual burnout, and personal stress. While Catholic clergy have been experiencing losses for years, mainline Protestants, including Presbyterians and Episcopalians, are no longer attracting leaders under the age of thirty-five. According to Darrin Patrick's research, "Eighty percent of seminary and Bible school graduates who enter the ministry will leave the ministry within five years" (Darrin Patrick, *The Life and Death of the Missional Leader*, First Session at May 2006 Resurgence Conference).

Without healthy leaders who have compelling vision, change will be very difficult.

- **Fact #7: The vast majority of American Christians currently give very little.** In fact, "at least one out of five American Christians—20 percent of all U.S. Christians—gives literally *nothing* to church, para-church, or nonreligious charities" (Smith and Emerson, *Passing the Plate,* 29). Even those with higher incomes do not give more in percentage. The little that is given is not spent much on poverty relief, missions, or human development, but on the local needs of their local church. Mass consumerism is driving the lives of most believers. "In 1920, the percentage of giving to missions from the total offering was 10.09 percent, just over a dime out of every dollar. In 2003, conservative and evangelical denominations gave 2.6 percent (about three cents per dollar), with the liberals giving only 0.9 percent (one cent). The combined average for overseas work is about two pennies per dollar" (Gene Edward Veith, "Who gives two cents for missions?," *WORLD*, Oct. 22, 2005, http://www.worldmag.com/articles/11176). While churchgoers do donate more for local relief for the poor than their unchurched peers, the poor themselves give more in percentage of their income than churchgoers.

We who have been given so much ought to be the first to give to others, even to the point of giving our very lives.

- **Fact #8: New forms of church are attracting the younger generation.** Pollster George Barna indicates a revolution is already taking place within the church, where approximately two-thirds of the nation's adults still attend. However, by 2025, "the local church will lose roughly half of its current 'market share' and . . . alternative forms of faith experience and expression will pick up the slack" (Barna Update, October 10, 2005). While not leaving the faith, growing numbers are leaving the institutional church in favor of spiritual alternatives and fewer demands from church life. From house churches to marketplace gatherings to the Internet, the quest for spiritual community and wisdom is no longer focusing on church sanctuaries. "As mainline churches scramble to retain young people, these worshipers have gained attention by creating alternative churches in coffee bars and warehouses and publishing new magazines and Bibles that come on as anything but church" (John Leland, *New York Times*, May 6, 2004). "A study by the Barna Group, a firm specializing in data on religion and society, estimates that 6 million to 12 million Americans attend house churches. A survey last year by the Pew Forum found that 9% of American Protestants only attended home services" (USAToday [AP], July 22, 2010, http://www.usatoday.com/news/religion/2010-07-22-housechurch21_ST_N.htm).

The church isn't—and can't be—identified with particular buildings but with a people led by God's Spirit.

It might be easy to become discouraged after reading these somewhat alarming trends and facts. But trends aren't prophetic certainties—they simple describe realities in our changing culture that can and must be acknowledged and addressed by any congregation that is slipping deeper into ill health. No church can respond to these challenges with easy answers or quick fixes. But with a heavy dose of reality and a reliance on Christ, any local congregation that knows it is called by God to be salt and light in the world can change and, in the process, become a powerful agent of God's kingdom.

The Examination Is Over—Now What?

Does the existence of your church really matter to anyone outside your congregation?

Before holding up your fists to defend your church, take a breath and answer that question as honestly as you can. Why does your church exist? Who cares if it exists? What would change if it didn't? Would the loss of your church harm your neighborhood or city? The painful truth for many American congregations is that little would change if they disappeared. What we can call "maintenance-driven churches" (Bandy, *95 Questions to Shape the Future of Your Church*, 9) are primarily concerned with their own survival and therefore aren't able to care about—and transform—the surrounding community.

Like the Americans who avoid an annual physical checkup, most churchgoing Christians never seriously consider a checkup of their own church, perhaps because they fear the results. What we need to remember, however, is that checkups have a vital purpose: *to make sure that we're healthy and that we stay that way.* While many churchgoers see and discuss things they like and dislike about their congregation, there seems to be a widespread aversion to any kind of organized effort to look at the various components of church health for the purposes of diagnosing and then curing problems. But in a church, as in a body, good health and peace of mind don't come from ignoring the warning signs.

But even if we agree that our church needs a checkup, who gets to decide what symptoms to look for and how to treat them? The parent of a teenager might focus on the health of the youth program, while a Sunday school teacher may examine the health of the church's Bible study habits. The list of church systems is almost endless: music, physical building, missions, budget and giving, teaching, staff, special services, community outreach, attendance, discipleship, and so on. Almost any of these could need some work, to say nothing of how they are working together as a whole. Looking at the whole body is difficult, and few experiences are more devastating than thinking we are doing well—only to find out that disease is lurking in the shadows.

We *must* take stock of the health of the American church. Church attendance continues to drop. Only half of American congregations are growing, and much of that growth is presumed to be transfer growth. Fewer than one in five Americans attends church—and these are usually "inspirational middle-class" churches that are family oriented and peopled with well-educated suburbanites. Disease *is* lurking in the shadows, and simply ignoring it and hoping it will go away is only going to make things worse.

How Did We Get Here? A Little Family History for the Chart

The people of God have a history of wandering and forgetting. The Old Testament describes how the children of God were frequently saved from their enemies by God's grace and mercy, only to forget their Rescuer and return to the captivity of other allegiances. This cycle—captive, crying out, delivered, compromising, forgetting—repeated itself countless times, and the church today is no different. We meander in and out of God's will, forgetting the basic lessons and principles of Scripture. Like lost sheep, we stray from the flock and must be found again and again.

It isn't that the truths of Scripture and what God asks of us are too complicated or esoteric. Indeed, it can even seem too simple: love God, love other people, and do these things wholeheartedly and faithfully. The New Testament often amplifies how renewal and restoration are constantly needed to live this out. We are called to "remain in [Christ]" (John 15), the source of faith, just as branches must abide in the vine from which they grow and receive their life.

Conversely, deadness and death are common images that describe what happens when we become detached from our source of life. Jesus curses the fig tree that does not produce figs. The New Testament reminds us how chasing good works and righteous requirements in our own power can quickly seduce us into worry, causing us to pursue what pagans chase (Matthew 6), to compromise morally (Romans 1), or to become hypocritical or double minded (James 1). We can think about Judas's betrayal, Peter's denial, Ananias and Sapphira's duplicity, Agabus's greed, the pride and external religion of the scribes and Pharisees—all of theses stories remind us of the brittle barrenness that awaits us when we try to do even the simplest of things without the power and perspective of God. The church is nothing less than loving God and loving each other with everything we've got.

It's the sometimes shocking gap between that simple truth and what we actually do that is so disturbing. The church has always needed checkups to ensure its health, and each generation confronts new symptoms. The church has trekked into remote, disease-infested villages to bring peace and healing, and the church has slaughtered countless thousands of Muslims beneath the banner of the cross. We have fed the hungry around the world, and we have erected wildly expensive and elaborate buildings in which to meet. The church has bridged geography and culture with the unifying good news of Jesus, and the church has idolatrously wrapped itself in the flag of patriotic nationalism.

In many ways the present condition of the church is just a mirror image of our own sinfulness. The church consists of sinful people; and it has been, is, and will continue to be sickened by our sin. The health of our future depends on the Healer and on our willingness to receive his healing and guidance. Renewal, rebirth, and reform are gifts of the Spirit. As we submit our churches to a much-needed checkup, let's remember that both the diagnosis and the cure are in the capable hands of the One who called the church into being and will one day welcome it into eternity as a perfect community.

PRESUPPOSITIONS

CHAPTER TWO

PRESUPPOSITIONS

If you don't change your beliefs, your life will be
like this forever. Is that good news?
—W. Somerset Maugham

The Church Wake

It was both a reunion and a funeral of sorts. Six friends who
had grown up in First Church vowed to meet on Labor Day
weekend every three years to maintain their friendship. This
gathering of former church members—and now their growing
families—had become a deep and meaningful event through the
years. The meeting place was the memorial plaque surrounded
by park benches, just one block off the downtown square in their
old hometown, the same place they had met for the last fifty-one
years. It was the site of some of their fondest memories as teens
and young adults. It was also the site where most of them had
experienced God's love and had been discipled to live out their
faith. And it was certainly a place where they had become the best
of friends. But now in the year 2031, things were very different.

It was almost 1:00, and one by one cars began to fill the nearby parking lot. Jerry had been waiting for an hour. Since his army days, he was early for everything. Now in their early seventies, he stood to watch them get out of their vehicles, no easy task as old age had made its mark. One had a cane, another a wheelchair, but most just shuffled across the street. The exception, of course, was Curtis, who at age seventy-one was still jogging each day. He jaunted across the street like a thirty-year-old. "Hey, buddy," said Jerry, "glad you could come back and remind us how out of shape we are! It's good to see you!"

By 1:40, all five friends had arrived—and the sixth wouldn't be coming. Handshaking, introductions, and humorous barbs filled the next twenty minutes. "How ya doing, honey?" said Marilyn as she hugged Anna, Ray's new bride of six months. "Hope you didn't have to be forced into the car to join our rendezvous," fully aware that reunions can be painful for those who married into this bunch and had to listen to exaggerated stories all weekend. From accounts of winning the district football game on the last play to confessions of how they poked holes in Brother Ed's waders on Sunday before he baptized new converts, she knew that much of their time together would be spent rehashing tall tales they'd all heard several times. "As the only girls in the reunion, Frieda and I will try to guard you against their propped-up egos and failing memories," said Marilyn.

The next hour was filled with lively conversation, laughter, and pictures of children, grandchildren, and even a few great-grandchildren. Any bystander could see the depth of their friendships by just watching from a distance. These men and women loved each other in a way that most people longed for. They had been on church retreats together, sung in the youth choir, and even attended Sunday night services and Wednesday night prayer meetings.

Those deep relationships began right on that very corner where the redbrick sanctuary used to stand. Five of the six came to First Church as babies and stayed active until they left for college or the army. Frieda had joined the youth group as a high school student, but she quickly broke into their circle with her amiable personality. For more than fifty years, they had remained friends, remembering birthdays and attending the weddings of each others' kids.

Except for Norm. After his alcoholism got the best of him in his twenties, he lost contact with almost everyone, including his family. Jobs came and went, and with no money or support system, he got into some legal trouble for drinking while driving and eventually ended up on the streets after a brief time in prison. Life had fallen apart for him, and he had never returned to the reunion since the first meeting. No one seemed to know what had happened to him. Curtis was the first to bring up his name, and then everyone's countenance changed from smiles to concern. But after a few solemn moments, the conversation moved on.

"Kind of sad isn't it?" said Marilyn. "Sitting here in front a memorial stone dedicated to the church that brought us together—I would have thought our funerals would have come long before the church's! I thought institutions never died."

"Yeah, guess I've never really been to a church funeral," mused Curtis. "But it's not like it was any surprise. Every time we met here, the signs of death seemed imminent. We've been watching this old place get more feeble than most of *you*," he needled, subtly reminding them of his fitness. "Knocking the old building down seemed to take it out of its misery! At least there's a nice new plaque!"

Ray lamented, "Seems like the more the world changed, the more they stayed the same. It's hard to believe how much life and excitement we used to experience here. I would have never guessed in a million years that the centerpiece of our community would shrink to the size of a plaque. It kind of makes you wonder if it could happen to all the other churches in town."

"It was those stinkin' liberals!" blurted Jerry, his voice filled with anger that surprised the group. "When they took the American flag off the stage, put drums in the worship service, and started forcing us into small groups instead of Sunday school, I could see it coming. You don't mess with what's worked for centuries. This church died because it didn't stay true to its traditions, which worked quite well."

Frieda took exception. "Jerry, I struggled with some of those changes, too, but I think the issue was a lot deeper than drums or a flag. This church became too judgmental. Remember a few years ago when Brother Ed organized the antigay march right there in front of the courthouse? Young people quit going to the church after that, and it began to shrink because they saw the church for what it was *against* instead of what it was *for*."

Jerry's voice trembled with anger. "So what's so wrong about that? The church is supposed to stand up against those idiots who promote gay marriage and kill unborn babies. That's what it's all about!"

"Hang on, Jerry," said Ray. "I agree that the church should have a strong ethical base, but it seems to me that Jesus loved folks who were immoral and nonreligious. In fact, if I can remember my Sunday school lessons correctly, he hung out with a prostitute, an antigovernment rebel, and financial criminals. Didn't they call him 'a friend of sinners'?"

Feeling uncomfortable with the tone and argumentation, Marilyn tried to redirect the focus and turned back to Frieda. "I don't know, Frieda. I've lived here all my life, and the church was always a great place for families to raise their children, even until the end when the doors were finally locked. We had a few bumps along the way, sure, but I think people have just become too busy and unspiritual. The problem wasn't the church; it was the culture. If people would make the church a priority again, things would be much better in the world."

"Better put me in that group of the unspiritual," chimed Curtis. "I got tired of old sermons that never had anything to do with my real life. I had more honest spiritual discussions with my softball team than with my Sunday school class. They may have used a few cusswords and drank beer, but my jock friends seemed to be more full of life and honest searching than our church ever was. I got tired of dressing up and playing church. Life is too short to go to a bunch of meetings and play like everything is hunky-dory. There were some really messed-up people here attending every week who smiled and acted like everything was just fine. But we all knew the things that were really going on. Don't forget the chairman of the deacons we all knew divorced his wife after having affairs, and no one ever processed that out loud with us. And remember our Sunday school teacher who was found dead from an overdose of sleeping pills. Why didn't anyone ever get honest around here? We were all messed up, but we never talked about it. I may be one of those unspiritual folks, but I've learned a lot more about being honest with myself than I ever did in church. Which brings me back to our own shortcomings. Any reason we've never gone to find Norm?"

"He's just an old penniless drunk," spouted Jerry.

Ray shot back, "Hey, wait a minute, old friend. Before we start picking on Norm, maybe each of us should do a little confession. Curtis is right. Have any of you ever gone looking for him after all these years? Seems like we all abandoned him after life got so tough. If the church stood for anything, it was that we should love each other and go looking for the lost sheep who strayed away. I'll admit my own failure to be his friend. Though I'm not so sure what I believe about the church anymore, I do think we've done a lot of talking and not so much walking with our faith through these years."

"It's his own fault," mumbled Jerry, "and I have no reason to go looking for him."

"I've talked with him," said Frieda. "A few years after our first meeting, I was meditating early one morning and really sensed *something* leading me to go find him. It took me several weeks to chase him down through the Web, phone calls, and other leads. He's right here in our hometown."

"Are you sure?" asked Marilyn. "I haven't seen him after living here all these years. Why didn't you ever tell us?"

"I'm not sure. And honestly, he really didn't want me to tell you all, since he felt like he had disappointed everyone with his addiction and bad choices. But he's doing great. I saw him again this morning before coming over here. You'd be proud. He ended up as the director of the homeless shelter that he once stayed in. God has been using him for years to help others who have struggled."

Anna, who had been silent during the entire conversation, finally broke in, ignoring the focus on Norm. "Frieda, is your meditation part of some new religious thing you are doing?"

"Well, sort of. I still believe in God, even Jesus and all that, but the more I learned about other religions, the more I came to believe that somehow they all go together. There are lots of ways to find God."

"Wow!" exclaimed Ray. "Anna and I have both wondered that ourselves. The more we traveled, the more we were exposed to other worldviews. I find myself struggling between what I was taught here at this church as a kid and my adult experiences. I wish we had been given a little more meat to consider back then, instead of worrying about how the black folks were going to be bused to our schools."

"Don't get me started on that topic," said Jerry.

Several of them laughed and were glad he chose to restrain himself. Like so many folks in those days of racial strife, the issue had divided many of them.

Curtis jumped back to the concern for Norm. "Frieda, you mean to tell me that after all the pain and mess of his life, Norm is a recovery counselor in a shelter and helps others there? That's amazing! Isn't it crazy how God can take us with all our scars and mistakes and still use us for good to serve others?"

All nodded in agreement, since they each had their own hidden scars.

Ray said what several were thinking deep down. "I wish we could revive this old church with that kind of honesty. Wouldn't it be great if we had a chance to take what we know about life now and reshape our old First Church into a bunch of Christians who could really make a difference with each other and the culture? I know we would probably disagree on a lot of things, but it seems like most of us still believe in the church and know God can still use it; we could tackle those differences and listen to each other enough to do this right."

"I'm still not letting you put drums in my new church," poked Jerry.

"Yeah, we know," laughed Ray. "If we make you chairman of the new church board, this will probably be our last reunion since we'll have to kill you!"

"Hey, let's take a break from talking," said Curtis. "How about we go find Norm and see if he'll join our newly formed committee? I'd love to see that ol' coot! Anyone want to go with me?"

As they got in their cars to follow Frieda to the homeless shelter, anxious to reunite with their old friend, they each silently wondered if they had somehow been a part of the death of their own church—and what should have been done differently.

What's Your Part?

In the story above, who did you most identify with? Who frustrated you? Did any of the characters remind you of people you know today? What do you think each of them believes about the church?

Our backgrounds, beliefs, and experiences shape our worldview. The uniqueness of our lives gives a particular color to the lenses through which we look at life—a color that doesn't quite match anyone else's. In the story above, the six characters give us a way to begin thinking about the predispositions and prejudices that impact how we judge life.

- **Jerry ("civil religion devotee")**—He's a veteran who served his country and sees his country and his faith as inextricably linked. He believes that liberal ideas and values have destroyed the American way and hurt the church; Jerry is convinced that the church is losing its own soul from cultural compromises, such as contemporary music, informal dress, and a lack of patriotism. He has come to believe that God blessed America materially because we had been faithful as a God-fearing nation. In fact, Jerry believes that we are a kind of "chosen people" that God wants to use as his instrument for right in the world. He resents the legal changes in society that have given rights to those he does not agree with. Jerry believes that the church must get back to its "old-time religion" if it is going to survive.

- **Marilyn ("loyal traditionalist")**—Her consistent church involvement from "cradle to grave" shaped her life. She has reaped the benefits of an era of good church programs and caring Christians who loved her and invested in her life. While she doesn't agree with all the changes, she is loyal to the local church and believes even the institutional model can be maintained in the culture. Marilyn tries not to think too much about problems or the possible need to change but prefers to "just do what is right." She wants everyone to get along and had a very hard time emotionally when First Church had to finally close its doors. She moved on to the smaller church near her house and is now leading the women's program there.

- **Curtis ("wanderer")**—He represents the large numbers who became disenchanted with the hypocrisy and shallowness of the local church and found "better" things to do on Sunday morning. While he finds escape in sports and leisure, he does recognize there is more to life than he is experiencing, but he can't find it in organized religion. Curtis still enjoys engaging in substantive conversations with friends, especially those who seem to be genuinely honest and interrogative. He is not mad at the church, but he feels like it lost its way and will probably never be the center of things that really matter in life.

- **Ray ("questioner")**—He tends to wonder and explore life questions, looking for deeper answers through reading and travel. While he would likely say he believes in the teachings of Christianity, his wider experiences while traveling in other cultures with different worldviews have made him less dogmatic and more uncertain about previously held beliefs. He often finds himself enjoying the antagonist's role in small-group discussions with those he considers closed minded, though he is unsure of the answers. Ray is one of those people who really needed a place in the church to honestly ask hard questions and not be criticized for doubts or a lack of faith.

- **Frieda ("postmodern")**—She has slowly rejected a lot of her earlier beliefs and become more pluralistic and humanistic, while still able to appreciate the good things churches do. While she does not have a formal theology and may not even consider herself a Christian, she is more of a practical atheist who wants everyone to get along and help each other, without resorting to God. Frieda's exposure to other religious practices has caused her to conclude that there is no one way to God and that he will accept anyone who is searching for truth and trying to help others.

- **Norm ("wounded healer")**—He represents those who felt rejected by the church but rediscovered Christ through his AA group meetings. He is a sponsor to several other former addicts and enjoys service toward the poor and marginalized in the community. He especially came to appreciate the honesty of "broken sinners" like himself that he never experienced in the church. For Norm, the church has nothing to do with a building, and his Bible study group has become his own church. He avoids most discussions of doctrine that tend to divide people and focuses mostly on their searching for God and healing of broken relationships from the past. He is very tolerant of wherever people are morally, believing that accepting and loving them is the first priority. Since he experienced God's restoration, he knows it can happen to anyone.

Understanding our presuppositions can be extremely helpful for church members beginning the process of change. Let's look a little deeper at the beliefs and actions of our cast of characters and try to see how each character approaches the risks and rewards of inevitable change.

Civil Religion, Family Holidays, and Being Nice

In Jerry's world, Christian religion and traditional American culture were different threads in the same fabric. God had blessed our nation because our nation trusted God and vice versa. As the wealthiest nation in the world, it was easy to assume God favored our nation above other nations and saw us as the "favored child." The Christian way of life and the American middle-class way of life were virtually the same, including being a decent parent and a responsible citizen. But the next generation, called the "boomers," saw little need for what some called "religion wrapped in a flag," and it exited the church for a variety of reasons. While the dangers of civil religion have been well documented, for Jerry it is the "liberals," those who do not share his views of religion and society, who are the problem. "Give me that ol' time religion" is his plea, since he only remembers how much the hymns and programs meant to him as a teen. The American culture began falling apart when the hippies of the Vietnam War era burned the United States' flag and rejected guys like him who returned from a war fought to defend their nation. The only way back is patriotism and hyperconservative values.

While most anyone who travels or keeps up with world events tends to see the positive values and privileges of the American culture, civil religion takes these blessings to another level. Like syncretism, which blends two disparate views into one, civil religion takes the American values and mixes them with Christianity. While in some cases there are commonly shared principles, in other areas American and Christian values actually collide. Since few churches seem to ever have honest discussions about these polarized differences, it becomes natural to blend them, as in Jerry's case.

However, when churches can discuss how the kingdom of God is uniquely different from the popular culture, then young disciples can explore their own views. For example, loving our enemies and doing good to those who hurt us are basic teachings of Jesus. Yet, many patriotic American Christians seem to hate all Muslims, who have been lumped together as "terrorists." Jesus' tolerance to engage in genuine conversation with the prostitute at the well and with unscrupulous tax collectors stands opposed to our lofty rejection of those who live immorally. We often forget that Jesus condemned the zealous Pharisees for their legalism, while frequently engaging in relationships with the rejected sinners of the day. Kingdom thinking recognizes servanthood as a higher value than control and understands that some things a culture values—even a good culture—must die so that the kingdom can grow.

For churches to honestly challenge cultural norms with biblical truths, there must be a place for open dialogue, and even disagreement, in the local church. Otherwise people like Jerry will never be able to reconsider how their allegiance to the nation may have compromised their allegiance to following Christ.

Jesus

Churchianity

In Marilyn's worldview, the church has been a faithful haven of support and encouragement her whole life. From "cradle to grave," the role of the church is to nurture and affirm those who are faithful to it. While she struggles some with Jerry's zealous patriotism, she struggles more with Curtis's abandonment of the church and Frieda's pluralism. Involved in Bible studies, homeschooling, and church choir, she felt her primary roles as wife and mother blended well in her church circles. "If everyone just got involved in the church, they would be better for it, and the churches would not be experiencing all these problems."

Marilyn has identified the church with the building and all its institutional programs. The idea of a church outside the walls seems weird, even cultic, for her. While she can acknowledge that the early church met in homes, she has never considered that church is about deep, world-changing community more than choirs and Sunday school. Her view of church has become so institutionalized that it is hard for her to see the benefits of anything but a highly organized approach, which provides her with clearly defined tasks and a sense of purpose and responsibility. She is a helper, who finds meaning in getting meals prepared for funeral guests and getting coffee ready for the Sunday school hour. Marilyn struggles with any talk about meeting in small, intimate groups that might make her more vulnerable, and with any suggestions that all members of the church are called to go into their communities and jobs in order to bring transformation and healing.

Just Do It

Curtis got tired of all the talk and hypocrisy. While he had been a tither and attender most of his life, one day he woke up and decided he didn't need the church. He felt like he had a genuine relationship with Christ, was relatively moral, and found fellowship with other "weekend warriors" who did everything from ride motorcycles to work in their lawns. Ironically, he discovered a lot of the new friends he hung around were just as "spiritual" as his old church friends. In fact, in many ways they were more honest and asked good questions about life. They even helped out in community fundraisers for local needs his church never seemed to care about. Curtis was not mad at the church. He just didn't see a need for it anymore.

Curtis was a relational guy who believed meaningful encounters were more valuable than most of the shallow relationships he had experienced in church. To him, Jesus had an incredible way of loving his disciples and also of challenging them with truth. Church folks seemed to be nice and polite and talk some about lofty ideals, but they struggled to get honest and be real. He had found his softball team and running buddies to be at least as real as the church folks, and he even found several of the guys who would talk deeply about their marriages, kids, and struggles at work—and the conversations often led to reflections about God. He found that he wasn't judged by them as much as he was by his former Sunday school class when he would occasionally talk about a personal problem.

Guys like Curtis flourish in small-group settings. If the church had been able to establish a small group that met weekly in homes, he would likely have never left. For the church to survive and grow, it must find a way to establish and sustain these relationship-based cells that nourish members, include outsiders, and provide service to the wider community.

The Seekers

When his first wife died, Ray started asking questions about God, the church, and everything else. He went through a difficult time of struggling to believe in anything, especially God. While his church was very hospitable and supportive in the days after her funeral, he now did not seem to fit, especially in "couples' classes." Gradually he pulled away from the church, but his faith experience heightened as he explored the harder issues of life, death, meaning, and purpose. He read everything he could find that interested him. He got involved in continuing education classes at the community college and took a few group travel trips to Israel, India, and Thailand to learn more about other worldviews. Eventually, Ray met a woman on the last trip who shared his interests as a learner and seeker, and they were married earlier in the year. Both still consider themselves Christians and found a new church to attend in their hometown, but their real joy is their small group, which meets weekly to talk and explore life.

Ray had a unique mix of Curtis's desire for honesty and Frieda's search for more meaning. While he covers his ambivalence with a dignified professionalism, he is the symbol of so many churchgoing folks who are deeply respected. Since he has seen the needs and faith practices of so many in the world, he really wants to live out the rest of his life making a difference. At one level he is deeply mission minded, but at the same time he questions his own views about the exclusivity of Christianity, which claims to be the only true way to God. His confusion occasionally is exposed in satire when he hears someone at church make an unloving judgment about another faith. The irony is that Ray would be the missional leader of the church if it could move past what he sees as pettiness. Even with his questions, he has the gifts of leadership and experience to mobilize a church to care for the poor in the community and practice Christian community development in other countries. He wants to deepen his faith and serve others, but he isn't sure that the local church has all the answers.

Stew-Pot Religion

Perhaps because her parents never attended church, Frieda never seemed to have that deep commitment to the church that the others did. After moving off to college, she quit attending, but she had numerous late-night discussions on the meaning and purpose of life in the dorm and sorority house. "I'm not sure how it all fits together," she would say, "but somehow I just believe all these different religions all fit together harmoniously in God's tapestry. I can't believe that there is one single way to God." She particularly lamented the antihomosexual and antiabortion judgmentalism she had observed as a young adult during several rallies. The "God hates fags!" banners and the news video of pro-lifers cheering after an abortion doctor had been shot seemed to have been the last straws. She believed in Jesus and knew him as a kind and compassionate teacher, but she had come to believe there were truths in other world religions that were also beautiful and that could help her life.

Frieda represents the growing number of fragile churchgoers who did not grow up in the church and have a hard time understanding the traditions and expectations of being a "good Christian." While she quit going to a formal church service, she had been invited several times to a local coffee shop where both young and old folks would have vibrant discussions around topics of faith, values, and God. It was fascinating to her to meet some in the group who were Christians and who were so willing to listen to others who did not share their views. They seemed to be intelligent people who could give a reasonable explanation to others in the group who pushed them for answers about the divinity of Christ or if God would really send those who didn't believe in him to hell. They didn't openly reject her Zen meditation practices, but they talked about how King David meditated with God in a different way. Most of all, she was enthralled that several of them had decided to live close to one another in a marginalized neighborhood so they could spend more time together helping their community. Frieda would never join a traditional church, but she is certainly open to learning and serving with Christians, provided the atmosphere is welcoming and nonjudgmental.

Least of These

Norm's life had gone down a rocky path. After his early years fighting "booze and crack," he came to the end of his rope literally, as he tried to commit suicide. His unsuccessful attempt forced him into a detox center and then counseling. Treatment was hard since he had never faced his inner pain from an abusive childhood. While he had been one of the most enjoyable students in First Church's youth group, no one seemed to be able to really get to know him. He had learned to hide his hurt and low self-esteem behind endless sarcasm and joking. After a year of community college, Norm dropped out of everything. As he slowly faced his childhood nightmares with his counselor, he came to understand the Higher Power as the living God who had walked with him and felt every pain of his past. The liberation of forgiveness and healing was deeply redemptive and life changing. While he continued to go to therapy and AA groups, Norm found the most strength from serving at the homeless shelter. He seemed to understand their struggles in a way that only one who had also hurt could know. Both the clients and the staff came to love and affirm him in ways he had never known, not even in the church. He was the obvious choice for the director's position when it opened up. After years of faithful service and unique administrative skills, Norm became the shelter's executive director. Five nights a week, he joined the men in the evening chapel services, discovering a depth of worship and thanksgiving he found nowhere else.

Norm's ability to relate to people with problems obviously came from his own experiences and feelings of failure. His recovery and healing had taken many years of digging out and confronting the pain from his childhood. But alongside the hours of therapy and following the Twelve Steps was the fellowship of friends who admitted they needed each other to survive. Breaking down the rugged individualism of our culture, they unashamedly talked about how a sponsor had confronted them or how getting honest in front of their peers had broken their hidden lifestyle. Like many who had maintained their sobriety, they had now moved from being served to serving others who were struggling. Norm even felt like it was almost unfair to pay him to do what he felt called by God to do.

There are so many people in the church who have much to offer our hurting world. Instead of helping and training and sending them, the church often holds them back from their calling. For the church to be what it is called to be in the world, congregations must find ways to affirm and send out the believers in their midst to where they are most needed.

Seeing God's Tapestry

Perhaps the most amazing thing about the church is God's vision that his people with wildly different personalities and backgrounds become a unified body as a sign of his kingdom. How can a man like Jerry share the Christian journey with someone as different as Frieda? We all seem to have such different presuppositions, experiences, and abilities that representing God in the world is a fantasy.

Doesn't history show that we have brought more dishonor to God's name with our disunity? Even the reality that churches are dying is a painful reminder that God seems to have made a bad choice with us.

Yet perhaps not. What if God's intention all along was to take a messy bunch of strugglers with countless differences and mold them into a single family called the body of Christ? Paul told the childish Corinthian church to quit fighting and acting immaturely, and instead recognize that the body is a unit, though it is made up of many parts (1 Corinthians 12). Our baptism brought opposites like slaves and free, Jews and Greeks, and rich and poor together as one. While we all have our different gifts and functions, we are part of the same body, which God can coordinate for his own glory. If we can simply recognize that God is our source, then people as different and frustrated as our reunion friends can find fulfillment and purpose in the same church. While certainly not an easy task, it is God's uncompromising call to us. And as we acknowledge and affirm each other's roles in that call, we become the hands and feet of God in a culture that needs God's body more than ever.

While the culture does not have the final word about the shape of the church, we must learn to listen to those we have been trying to "save" from that culture. Listening is hard, especially when we try to listen to those who do not share our values or beliefs. It means hearing the perceptions of the church from those outside it—with humility, grace, and love. It means asking what those views mean for our local congregation.

Some believe we should remove ourselves from the culture, rejecting fads, techniques, and trends. Others say just the opposite: we should embrace the cultural patterns and make Christianity more tenable for folks who reject the church of the twentieth century. Still others believe we can transform the culture into God's image and for his purposes.

Struggling churches must look reality squarely in the face and ask: What is God's call? They must recognize that the personalities of our reunion group represent real people, not just fictional characters. Their members and those who have already left the church in anticipation of its death have different personalities and views. Some are entrenched in the traditions of the church, while others have been looking around in other places for truth to fill the void. Facing reality means two things: First, if the church is going to survive, it must be committed to unity, despite the inevitable differences. Second, there will be different ways God leads churches to be on mission in his world and in the culture. Being open to hearing God's unique call is crucial.

The world is a big place, and there is always room for different expressions of God's church in that world. For example, a church could support Norm in the homeless shelter while also helping Curtis establish a small house church. They could mentor and disciple Frieda to lead a different discussion group in another location where unchurched folks go. Jerry's church could bless him to be a pastor to the veterans who fought for our country and still weep when they see the American flag. Marilyn will continue to be a superstar church member, serving within the body, but gradually learn to be honest in a small group. Ray and Anna could be affirmed as the missional directors of their church and given the task of mobilizing church members to do local and international mercy ministries.

There are no formulas to help churches change successfully. Relationships are messy, especially when things are tough, and every church is built on relationships. Yet Peter says we are a royal priesthood and a holy nation (1 Peter 2:9) for God's purposes. If God created the universe and designed the church, who are we to limit the ways God wants to use us in our culture?

the churchianity? United? What is true?

Keeping churchianity (the body of Jesus? They need to be ready to obey Jesus, the Gospel even thing they are very different.

PURPOSE

CHAPTER THREE
PURPOSE

The church exists for nothing else but to draw
men to Christ, to make them little Christs.
—**C. S. Lewis (*Mere Christianity*)**

Let's get down to business: What *is* the church, anyway, and what should it look like?

If a church is going to pass through the fires of change to become something different, it must work through its understanding of what the Scriptures say about the body of Christ and subsequently decide what model or models best capture the essence of what it means to be a church.

Deep and Wide

"You were made for mission. God is at work in the world, and he wants you to join him" (Warren, *Purpose-Driven Life*, 281). The core identity of the church is this: the people of God are an extension of Christ, loving God and each other wholeheartedly, and acting as a sign of the reign of God, both now and in the coming kingdom. That is what it means to be made by God for mission in the world.

This mission is a deeply integrated fusion between inward and outward living. While such a claim may sound merely theological or abstract, in practice the inward-outward fusion requires us to live purposely and presently in our neighborhoods. Elizabeth O'Connor and the Church of the Savior in Washington, D.C., embodied this. Under the leadership of Gordon Cosby, the congregation in an impoverished, urban neighborhood promoted incarnational living to transform the community, as well as two-year study courses and regular spiritual disciplines. When asked about the integration of the outward and inward, O'Connor reflected that the "movements must not be separated. . . . [I]f we use our work simply as a further quest for self, then we will lose it and go backward. But if churches can provide a place where people can be on an inward journey but also model the outward, people will naturally flow from the inward to the outward. I think they don't because we don't show them how" (*Faith at Work Magazine*, 1977).

The church has always had this unified purpose, regardless of how successfully it was accomplished—or if it was even acknowledged! Individual churches have always swung between the two poles of inward and outward, whether moving into separatist or contemplative isolation or pushing members to evangelistic street campaigns in their local communities. From one end of the continuum to the other, making sense of the inward-outward tension has always been challenging. In our current North American context where the attractional model of church —a model centered on simply getting people to come to church— is primary, we are beginning to see the momentum swing toward outward engagement and returning to our communities with good news. Yet even now as we move outward, we must be careful to keep God's holistic purpose in mind.

The children's action chorus "Deep and Wide" gets it right, integrating both genuine depth and wide action. Biblical principles such as confession, forgiveness, reconciliation, encouragement, and admonishment must connect with the local community where injustice and brokenness rule. There is a fountain flowing through the life of God's church that can transform all creation. To ignore either the members of the body or the neighborhoods and nations to which he sends us is to diminish the work of Christ. God is at work in the world, and in every heart, and God is calling the church to that same mission.

Real Change Springs from Internal Life

Churches that genuinely want to change cannot do so without serious reflection on their own spiritual formation. Biblical change is transformative. It converts us at many levels, including our loyalties, beliefs, personal biases, and attitudes. Such radical reorientation requires a spiritual compass capable of navigating when we can't see the goal clearly.

Piety is that spiritual compass, the essential guidance and practice that keeps us moving in the right direction. In common usage, piety has come to mean a willingness to be devout, reverent, and spiritually disciplined—particularly with reflective times of prayer, study, meditation, and fasting—to win the favor and forgiveness of God. Yet understood biblically, piety is not about being *spiritual* at all—it's about being *whole*. And without real piety, local churches struggling to transform will not succeed. The Hebrew people understood piety as reverence for God, including traits like respect, sacrifice, loyalty, devotion, and awe. To know God was to love God and do his will. Biblical piety begins with God's love, which draws us to him in intimacy. Spiritual disciplines do not get us to God; God's Spirit draws us to him in love, and from that relationship we hear the call to prayer, meditation, Bible study, fasting, simplicity, and obedience. When we understand piety this way, we see that it isn't a series of actions we add on to our lives to be "better"; instead, our actions are a natural response to the love of God as we become whole.

Even as the apostle John exposed the strengths and weaknesses of the seven churches in Revelation, the church must be able to see more clearly how God sees us so that we can make appropriate changes. Such introspection does not come easily in a culture that cannot "be still, and know that I am God." In the rush of life, it is virtually impossible to hear the voice of God amid the hundreds of other voices demanding attention. Only as we pull aside from "normal life" and make room for prayer, reflection, confession, community, and corporate worship can we hear that still, small voice that is the Spirit of Christ. Churches that genuinely want to change must create both personal and corporate opportunities for God to challenge our lukewarm hearts, complicity with the world, and loss of vision.

Throughout history, each time the church becomes rigid and dry from legalism, apathy, or shallowness, God's Spirit seems to eventually usher in the fresh winds of change to renew the hearts of followers who thirst for more than empty religion. Renewal movements emerged from God's call to the Pietists, Moravians, Reformers, Anabaptists, and leaders of the Great Awakening. These movements often created conflict with the established church that had grown powerful or set in its ways. Thousands of martyrs died, not only from outside persecution, but even from the swords of those within the church who resisted change. Yet for those who experienced God's deep call to the renewal of the bride of Christ, even fear of death was worth the risk.

Contemporary movements in the last century have continued to call Christians back to their "first love." Revivals, renewal conferences, Renovaré, New Monasticism, and national college gatherings like Passion have each brought unique challenge to Christians hungry for more than institutional religion that can often become lifeless and routine. Even as our pluralistic, postmodern culture is derailing traditional churches, those who have left the church are not abandoning their faith, but are seeking a deeper walk with God in new ways. If the average church is going to survive, it must be among a people where genuine seeking and spiritual growth can occur. Few believers today are interested in helping a dying church cling to life if there is little internal evidence of the Spirit present.

Real Change Impacts Outward Movement

Recently, as many traditional churches began to struggle with declining attendance and falling budgets, *renewal* became a buzzword. Enormous amounts of energy were spent on renewal, because many equated renewal with becoming healthy and believed becoming healthy would lead to an externally focused church.

Unfortunately, so-called renewal has little to do with health. If being focused on and active in the inward-outward mission of God is what it means to be a healthy church, a church going through a time of renewal may simply be entering a new phase of self-preservation—and subsequent self-focus. A church can increase its understanding of biblical leadership, help members identify their spiritual gifts, and deploy a more contextual style of music, but none of these will necessarily involve members in community-focused mission.

True renewal isn't about new programs or plans, but about the movement of God in believers' lives to transform the deadness brought by sin and disobedience. Only God "make[s] everything new" (Revelation 21:5), from the smallest church to worldwide movements of mission. Every church and every Christian manifests deadness differently, but the source of real rebirth is always the same.

A genuinely healthy church is a church that is clearly growing both internally and externally, though that growth does *not* have to be numeric. Rather, the growth is about what God seems to be doing for his beloved children who are both inside and outside the church. There are no formulas or steps. Healthy churches can be any size and any denomination. They can have any number of programs or no programs at all. They can have one pastor or one hundred pastors. However, there is one thing that is not optional.

A healthy church is always missional.

When a healthy church is participating in God's mission, the measurement of its health is the transformation of both the membership and the community. A healthy church is more interested in what God is doing in hearts, neighborhoods, and the world than with new strategies for growth.

The Attractional Church—Get 'em and Keep 'em

If a local church believes its *primary* purpose is to get the community into the building, that church is operating as an attractional church. For such churches, the most important goals tend to be focused on the maintenance of the church institution. Some of these goals include:

1. Good Leadership: Do the pastor and church staff help the church become more attractive to insiders and outsiders? Does the congregation feel "shepherded"?
2. Strong Attendance: Is the church growing numerically?
3. More Involvement: Are the church members getting more connected to Bible study, prayer groups, Sunday school, missions, and other programs in the church?
4. Meaningful Worship: Is there a good balance of preaching, singing, and fellowship that motivates the congregation to participate in the service? Does it meet the members' felt needs?
5. Christian Education: Are the children, youth, and adults learning the Bible and living morally?
6. Vision and Strategy: Does the church have an effective plan for future growth?
7. Good Organizational Structure: Is there a clear organizational chart, good lines of communication, building maintenance, and program delivery?
8. Contextual Missions (Global and Local Outreach): Is the church supporting and affirming those who have gone overseas or who are called to "home missions"?
9. Budget and Giving: Is the church meeting its annual budget?

In most growing attractional churches, the majority of these components are being achieved in acceptable ways. Areas of weakness are usually discussed, and the paid staff generally ensures the objectives are reached. The result of this process is a church that prioritizes, and often achieves, two things: numerical growth and satisfied members.

So let's ask ourselves: Is growing larger and more content what Jesus is calling his church to?

What's God Really Up To?

What if the purpose of the church has been diluted or distorted? When the pews are packed and the budget is in the black, few members ask this question. After all, aren't the various sorts of numerical growth evidence that we're getting things right? Sometimes this attitude trickles down, as televised megachurches control the center of attention with their unprecedented numbers, facilities, and social opportunities. Many smaller churches emulate these megachurches at whatever level they can afford, hoping that with enough time and strategy, any church can—and should!—become mega.

But the smell of death is in the air. Many smaller congregations can no longer compete with full-service church centers and marketing campaigns. The iconic hometown church with intact families sitting next to each other in their neatly pressed church clothes is becoming a picture of days past, like a Norman Rockwell painting. In their failed efforts to act like megachurches, many smaller churches have also failed to be a healthy, thriving *small* church as well. When this happens, the "loser" isn't the church building—it's the community that can no longer be transformed by the loving mission of those church members.

This death has been a long time coming. With the loss of the Hebraic holistic lens of the early church, the Western church, and especially its contemporary, North American iteration, began to separate the "spiritual" from everyday life. The first-century Greek heresy called Gnosticism suggested that *knowing*, not *doing*, was the essence of faith. Flash forward through the Middle Ages, the Enlightenment, and modernity, and we see churches that emphasize consumerism: meeting *my* personal needs and ensuring *my* personal salvation. People in the pews have become consumers of religious goods and services offered by the church.

Consequently, instead of following the biblical example of the Old Testament prophets, Jesus, Paul, and the other apostles and uniting our faith with missions and action, we have accepted a religion in which the only requirement is to be *nice*. We go to worship services with our families and avoid the vices of the culture and say all the right things—at least in public. Our churches focus on "getting people saved" so the people can go to heaven and the churches can grow. *Believing* is a requirement, while *doing* is optional—and sometimes even suspect. In this new form of Gnosticism, mere belief motivated by one's personal desire to go to heaven and avoid hell creates a simplistic formula for taking care of "spiritual things."

These subtle half-truths have done what no army could do to Christianity: subverted it and converted it from the inside out. The transforming good news has been diluted into a type of cheap grace. The biblical mandate to "take up your cross and follow" has been replaced by the institutional mandate of attractional churches to "sit in your pew and tithe." Is this now what we have to offer a world desperate for hope and transformation?

Kingdom of God

Thankfully, God's truths can never be destroyed, no matter how greatly we distort them or how strenuously we ignore them. In recent years, biblical scholars have reminded church leaders that giving his followers a free pass to heaven was not the foremost purpose of Jesus' teaching, death, and resurrection. From the beginning of his earthly ministry, he challenged everyone he met to perceive that "the kingdom of God is near." Salvation, biblically understood, was the gift of God for those who were willing to submit to his lordship and proclaim their Lord's reign that was now present and yet to come. It was the banner under which all nations and classes could assemble to make the "kingdom come . . . on earth as it is in heaven." It was, in fact, a revolutionary call to submit to no other gods but to the true and living God, who had conquered sin and death. Salvation was a summons for the church to put on the "full armor of God" and fight in kingdom ways for the kingdom.

That sounds a little different from individuals saying the "sinner's prayer," doesn't it?

The church is the visible body of Christ that exists for the sake of God's kingdom. Though not the kingdom itself, the church is God's witness to his current and coming reign. The "little flock" is to be a people who, living under Christ's lordship, act with his values and point to a better way—a good-news way of healing, hope, reconciliation, servanthood, and unconditional love.

Simply put, the church is God's agent for announcing the kingdom and declaring good news to a world that is estranged from his purpose and love. God's mission calls all creation to live under the "reign of God." Our reason to exist is to be God's hands and feet, his ambassadors, to love and serve a broken world and call it back to Jesus, the Savior and Lord of all. Through proclamation, acts of kindness, teaching, giving, serving, praying, and sending, the church of Jesus Christ exists to do the King's will, regardless of the cost. The King's purpose may not be for higher church attendance, a new building campaign, or an increasing level of comfort, but it will *always* be for his church to declare the good news of salvation—real, holistic, here-and-not-yet-here salvation.

The Missional Church: Get 'em and Send 'em

There are two Greek words in the New Testament for the English word "life." One is *bios*, or mere existence. The other is *zoe*, which means life full of meaning and purpose. God's intent for his creation is the latter. "I have come that they may have life, and have it to the full," the Scripture proclaims (John 10:10). How quickly the joy and zeal to live life fully become the drudgery of "just another day." While certain life circumstances magnify the challenges to live abundantly, the average Christian has no excuse for a routine, mundane, and bland life. With only one life to live, how is it that we accept drudgery as normative?

If we are going to ever find *zoe*, it will come at a price—but the very nature of abundant life means that it will be worth it!

Earlier we looked at the common priorities of an attractional church. Now, as we look at the priorities of a missional church, we need to remember a guiding principle: the only way for a church to be healthy and thrive—to have *zoe*, in other words—is to be on mission with God. Every other priority of a healthy church is built on this reality. All churches have the same mission, and while there are many styles and ways in which that mission can be accomplished, the underlying purpose never changes.

Historically, however, the church often loses its way, wandering off like a lost sheep from the shepherd's care. Congregations begin to redefine who they are based on denominational priorities, attendance goals, and building programs. In all the busyness of church activities, it seems there is rarely a meeting to ask the hard question, "Why do we exist?" Yet it is exactly through such self-examination that churches can begin to move back toward God's purposes and mission.

While not an exhaustive list, or even a prescriptive one, the following ideas can help us think about some characteristics of a healthy, missional church. All of these characteristics describe a church that is about God rather than a church that it is about itself.

1. A sense of kingdom-mindedness and vision in the congregation to be about God's purpose
2. A diverse group of church leaders who feel personally called and responsible to each other and the world
3. Listening opportunities for leaders to hear and affirm their members and build genuine relationships, including time to have fun
4. An outward focus on the larger community, including an awareness of the demographics and needs
5. A diversity of members from various economic, racial, and moral backgrounds who feel accepted and included
6. Respect for and dialogue with those who may not agree with church leaders and the church's direction
7. Care for the poor and marginalized of the community and the world
8. The physical presence of church members in the neighborhood, responding to community needs
9. Opportunities for spiritual formation that clarify God's call to the members
10. Training and affirmation of gifts that equip members for ministry
11. Welcomes outsiders regardless of background

12. Promotes small groups that engage and disciple, communicating love and encouragement

13. Speaks out against and acts to remedy injustice, locally and globally

14. Uses a culturally relevant and particular model that the unchurched can understand

15. Has flexible structures—buildings, staff, budget, and so on—that can change as the church becomes more missional

Unlike the traditional components of an attractional church that focus on self-maintenance and preservation, a missional church looks at health through a different lens. A missional congregation might ask, "Is more of our budget going to serve others or our own congregation?" "Is the leadership of the church equipping me to use my gifts to build up the church and help the community?" "Do we as a church have a strategic plan to reach out to and serve the unchurched and the poor and marginalized of our community?" "Does our worship cause me to see and examine my own unworthiness and need for God to empower me to do his will?" (Guder, *Continuing Conversion of the Church*, 155).

As an organism, a healthy church is a growing church— but that growth will not always be numerical. Eric Swanson, a missional leadership specialist with Leadership Network, says, "Becoming an externally focused church will lead to church growth. Being missional or externally focused always leads to kingdom growth, but not necessarily church growth" (Eric Swanson, personal e-mail, May 17, 2010). The Hartford Seminary study examined over fourteen thousand congregations and determined that churches that participated in social ministries and social justice "were more likely to be growing than other congregations" (Faith Communities Today, "The Compassionate Congregation," http://FACT.hartsem.edu, Hartford, CT, FACT study). Swanson and Rick Rusaw cofounded the Externally Focused Network to help train, motivate, and connect an exploding group of missional churches that are engaging in practical ways in local communities instead of concentrating on getting the communities to attend their worship services.

Purpose Drives Transition

"It's not about you. The purpose of your life is far greater than your own personal fulfillment, your peace of mind, or even your happiness" (Warren, *Purpose-Driven Life*, 17). If Rick Warren's words are true, much of what occupies our time and energy is secondary at best and sinful at worst. If we are living obediently, our purpose is singular—to live out God's will as the people of God. Any other church goals or dreams must be subservient to that. When a local church grasps this profound truth, its actions take on a different value. God really cares little about Sunday school and styles of worship compared to his passion for discipleship and worship. And while church decisions have practical implications, which do require a congregation to decide and implement, ultimately those decisions are secondary to God's purposes.

One of the most helpful exercises a church in the midst of change can do is to bring the congregation together around this issue. With some good leadership and basic ground rules, a four-week series, held once a week, to explore the purpose of the church will likely elicit myriad expectations of why the church matters. Certainly, some guided Bible study about what Scripture says about the body of Christ and its purpose is foundational. Following that meeting might come another one focused on cultural influences that have shaped today's congregations, along with candid opinions about how these have positively or negatively impacted the church's purpose. This would lead naturally into the age-old question of how members think the church should respond to today's society and its values. For example, some members may see the church as a "light on the hill," which is somewhat removed from culture and its trends but shines as a light in the darkness of sinful culture. Other members may think that the church should strive to be culturally appropriate, even adapting certain neutral lifestyles that make it more relevant to the changing culture. Still others might see the church's purpose as transformational in the lives and the existing structures of society, therefore wanting their congregation to be involved in school boards, city councils, and local neighborhood associations.

The moderator of these important discussions should make every effort to be sure various members are acknowledged as valuable and that the opinions are recorded. Eventually, these opinions reveal how local members of the congregation see their church's role, internally and externally. Some want the church to be a "hospital for sinners," while others want it to be a "fortress from culture's influence." Some will stress the church's responsibility to "take care of its own," while others may lobby for a mission-minded church that sends members to the field.

Some patterns will likely emerge suggesting the majority views, as well as the strong opinions of various influential members. While "majority rules" should not govern the next steps, the church must work to acknowledge the basis of these opinions, whether from its own experiences or biblical principles or both. No serious change can occur in any local church unless clarification of the church's purpose is reconsidered. As these discussions mature and members start to find common ground, the church can begin to move to the next level of discussion around the implications of that purpose, both locally and globally.

Christian Community Development

It's crucial to remember that the goal isn't to be *called* a missional church, but to change our church so that it can *do the things* that will make it missional. Being missional isn't about a label—it's about a way of living that grows God's kingdom of love and grace and empowerment in our communities and in the world.

While most churches recognize that word and deed are blended into a single holistic unit in the *Bible*, many have divided evangelism and social action, choosing to emphasize one as more important than the other—or to insist that one no longer matters at all!

Yet all around the country, diverse Christians from most every major city are discovering significant ways to unite word and deed. Churches are providing job training and creation, alcohol and drug recovery, prison ministry, racial and class reconciliation, transitional shelters, free clinics, literacy classes, affordable housing, and youth empowerment programs. They are tackling difficult issues of sex trafficking, fair trade, HIV/AIDS, hunger, clean water, prison reform, microloans, environmental injustices—right here and around the world—all as a part of their growing faith and holistic biblical understanding.

Churches that have moved outside of the walls of their buildings to forge relationships with the community are discovering a new level of compassion, outreach, and leadership.

Including those who are being served in the life of the church is rarely an easy transition. It is much easier to do "for" someone, especially when there is an immediate satisfaction, than to find ways to overcome different worship styles, dress, and cultural backgrounds. But "kingdom living" on earth is the foretaste of being eternally with the King. We are to practice the kingdom "on earth as it is in heaven." Such practices solidify congregational purpose. Not only are Christians in local churches becoming more intentional about their vocational callings, but the unbelieving world is awakening to recognize that the church is more than a gathering of homogeneous religious people who cluster together on Sunday morning. When non-Christians who have been critical of today's churches see people of all races, income levels, education levels, and diverse backgrounds worship together and love each other, they begin to see—as if for the first time—the good news of Christ. In fact, holistic community development, motivated by God's love, becomes a primary catalyst for evangelism to people who desperately need to "see" the gospel and not just hear empty rhetoric.

Consequently, many churches—in their quest to change and fulfill God's purposes in the world—are reshaping their infrastructure to serve those whom Jesus constantly served: the poor, the orphan, the widow, and the outcast. They are creating separate 501(c)(3) nonprofit organizations to better mobilize their members and handle funding needs and legal requirements. Some are discovering that home groups in diverse neighborhoods are dramatically more inviting to those who would never walk in the doors of a church building. And some are even finding that bars, dance halls, bingo parlors, and recovery meetings are ideal venues to build relationships with genuinely caring followers of Jesus.

"Adopting missional behaviors requires changes to a leader's weekly schedule in order to spend more time beyond the walls of the church building," concluded Dave DeVries ("Missional Transformation: Fueling Missionary Movements that Transform America"). He discovered what most of us intuitively know: only one-fourth of all Christians are spending time with unbelievers and people in need. Missional behavior means sharing meals, praying specifically for unbelievers, and addressing the needs present in every community. Such purposeful behavior is natural for a mission-oriented believer or church, but the process of changing into that sort of person or church can be painful and messy. Fortunately, that sort of change always begins in a place—the place where we live and work and worship—and understanding place will help us understand change.

mission: what kind of needs?

All of human life / polit, social, economic, edu.—

but we begin doing from healthy Christian spirituality

mission is the result of spiritual growth.

PLACES

CHAPTER FOUR
PLACES

We are in danger of making our cities places
where business goes on but where life, in its real
sense, is lost.
—Hubert H. Humphrey

Theology of Place

Historically, ever since the first purpose-built church structure was erected more than a millennium and a half ago, most Western Christians have worshiped God in the pews of traditional local church buildings. For many Christians, there is a profound sense of holiness experienced in these structures—whether a white wooden church in New England or a cathedral in the English countryside—that is rarely found outside the walls. Around the world, God is mysteriously present to many Christians in the brick and mortar, and the presence of the people of God within a building brings a collective emotional connection. For many Christians in America, this phenomenon still exists. From stained glass to steeples, religious symbols engender relationship with the living God.

Yet at the same time, a growing unchurched population does not connect church buildings with the sacred or the spiritual. Many in our postmodern culture feel little affinity toward church structures or religious symbols. In fact, for many of them who have grown resentful of "institutional religion"—or simply know little or nothing about the institutional church—religious buildings actually produce negative feelings. Christians are often seen as judgmental, negative, and hypocritical, and the "church house" is merely a collection of narrow-minded "God-talkers" who do little for society. Most of these critics still have a relatively high view of God and Jesus; they just believe that the Christians inside church buildings are not really "Christ followers."

That raises an obvious question: Can we be Christ followers with no buildings?

Third Places

Today's generation is adept at creating virtual places—online meeting areas where connection and interaction can occur. We're all familiar with the patterns of social networking forming around Facebook, Twitter, and YouTube, but even these opportunities haven't satisfied our need for *places* in which relationships can occur. In cities, at least, younger generations are building intentional communities in their own neighborhoods, implicitly rejecting the isolation of gated communities and suburbia. New Urbanism, community-supported agriculture (CSAs), and community houses are emerging as trends in response to our longing for place.

This longing for community and spirit of innovation is spilling over into the way Christianity is perceived and practiced. Rejecting—or at least ignoring—traditional church buildings, the unchurched still want meaningful relationships with those who encourage them, and they want to create an atmosphere of acceptance and comfort. In what some call "third places," real (not virtual) locations outside of home and work are sought where relationships can occur. Privatized lifestyles centered more and more around isolated computer screens and electronic social networks cannot consistently satisfy the longing for human relationships that take place face to face in the real world.

Therefore, a growing number of new places, sometimes called "third places," are emerging, from coffeehouses to bookstores to bars to garden shops—places that often take the place of traditional church buildings as groups of friends gather around a common interest. Third places become the location of life-changing discussions about life, purpose, values, politics, and death. It isn't only that Sunday school classrooms have been replaced because of the decline of traditional church *buildings*, but that Sunday school classrooms often seemed to push out real dialogue in favor of pat answers. And it goes without saying that these third places tend to be much more inclusive and welcoming than the average institutional church. Thus, it may not be a question of following Christ with *no* buildings, but of following Christ in different, more flexible buildings.

Crumbling Cathedrals

Today, the physical church building is one of the most challenging dilemmas for churches in crisis. Since most American churches have less than one hundred members, and many of them are older, keeping the doors of the building open has become a major challenge. Almost one-fifth of church budgets are used for debt payments, repairs, and maintenance in buildings that are used only a few hours a week. In fact, the cost of maintenance, repairs, and physical improvements frequently becomes the tipping point for a church that is already struggling to meet its budget and keep its staff. Tempers can flare when the cost of replacing air-conditioning units, old plumbing, and leaking roofs becomes the primary topic of meetings—not to mention that the mission and calling of the church become compromised. These budgetary decisions often force churches to acknowledge they have to either increase members and their budget or watch their church building and programs slide further into neglect. For many financially strapped churches, cutting staff and programs is the first line of defense to save the decaying building. However, such budget cuts rarely stop the bleeding.

The irony of the church building dilemma is that the church did just fine without any buildings of its own for the first three hundred years, meeting in homes. It was much later in history when churches began to identify themselves with buildings. Yet today, it is hard for active church members to even consider a church without walls, even if selling the property might bring a fresh start. The church building usually takes on a sacred role for long-term members who have invested deeply in it and enjoyed the convenience of a permanent location. Rarely do members recognize that the location, amenities, and structure display how a church views its purpose in the community. When we find ourselves more committed to the place than to the people—to each other, to our neighbors, to the persons of the Trinity—then our theology of place must be expanded.

The alternative is a continuing commitment to a specific, physical place—and a continuing shuffle toward irrelevance. Yet even that reality is in jeopardy, since it is the older generation that currently gives over three-fourths of the funds that keep the building intact, while the younger generation is no longer so committed to institutional buildings. In a growing consumerist culture where money becomes more sacred and private, congregations will continue to struggle to pay the bills unless their purpose is deeply shared by the next generation. The church is still alive, but it is likely that most of these crumbling cathedrals will be closed up in the years ahead.

Homes, Schools, and Public Places

Most church planters already understand the reality that new congregations almost always begin and grow in nontraditional settings. Many begin in homes and grow into other meeting places such as schools, hotels, storefronts, movie theaters, even other church buildings when they are not being used. These new churches often experience great freedom and potential growth because they are not encumbered by the debt and need for repairs that can plague traditional churches. While it may be emotionally painful for older church members who have tied their faith to a particular building, with patience and opportunities to grieve the loss even they can understand that change may be the only way for the church to grow and thrive again.

That's not to say that change is easy! One of the more difficult realities for established congregations is accepting the challenges of mobility after long years of having personal classrooms, closets, and permanent space. Setting up and tearing down chairs and sound systems requires extra time and energy that some members may prefer not to spend. Yet often those very challenges require corporate efforts to solve, and these can build friendships and unity.

I recently spoke in a school-based church that had purchased an entirely mobile setup for worship that could be assembled or taken down in thirty minutes. With precision, assigned teams set up chairs, the stage, tables, and music equipment to create a relatively warm worship atmosphere. After the service, everything was returned to designated and labeled customized containers, loaded into a trailer, and stored until the following week. Their church on wheels was fascinating and purposeful—and cost only a *tiny* fraction of a traditional church building. Church members clearly experienced a sense of teamwork and fellowship symbolic of the body of Christ, and the setup allowed them to scale up or down in different temporary meeting locations.

That sounds incredibly different from a traditional brick-and-mortar church—but doesn't it sound better in many ways, too? Like Christ himself, perhaps your church is being called to go *into* the world in a literal sense, instead of expecting the world to come to you.

Church under the Bridge

For the last nineteen years, I have been the pastor of a congregation that meets outside each Sunday morning under an Interstate 35 bridge in Waco, Texas. What began as a Bible study for a handful of homeless men and women who slept there eventually attracted college students and local residents. Today, over three hundred diverse members gather under the bridge each week. We serve meals, set up chairs and stage equipment, and even make portable toilets available. While there are certainly some inconveniences, the benefits far outweigh them. Even in colder weather, there is a sense of community when worshipers share blankets with each other, similar to a football game. We have monthly Communion, recovery group meetings, health fairs, weddings, and several worship services, and while overhead traffic does create a certain amount of noise, we have discovered a reverence for God in that unlikely place that is clearly worshipful.

One of the greatest benefits is our discretionary income. Since taxpayers paid for and maintain our concrete "building," we pay nothing for this creative worship center. That, and the fact that we have a smaller part-time paid staff, gives us the freedom to spend over half the church's financial resources on the physical and spiritual needs of the poor in our community and around the world. Since most church members today "give less than 2.5% of their income to the church and the vast bulk of it is spent on themselves" (Sider, *Just Generosity*, 92), little is left for the needs of the poor. Folks at our church tend to give with joy and generosity because they know their donations are making a direct difference in the local community and the world. We're giving up the comforts of owning our own building for the greater call of our faith—and we're having a blast doing it!

This visible, outdoor church has been an extraordinary witness to the community. Visitors show up weekly, sometimes in significant numbers and from all over the nation. A common space is now a holy space, and there is a natural curiosity evoked and a nonverbal invitation to come join this outdoor festival of faith. We are free to follow Christ and use the financial resources of our congregation for missional purposes.

Tabernacle and Sanctuary

Meanwhile, on the other end of the spectrum, what are called *megachurches*—churches with more than 2,000 members—are expanding. In some cities, construction of huge new sanctuaries is astounding. Driving by buildings like Lakewood Church in Houston, Texas, with 43,500 members, or Life Church in Edmond, Oklahoma, which houses over 26,000 members, creates a visual sense that the Christian church is exploding in America.

It is true that these churches appear to be flourishing. Recent research by the Hartford Seminary Institute suggests that they are doing a relatively good job of reaching, keeping, and engaging their members. Most of these congregations have younger members and more single members than traditional churches, and two-thirds of their members have been attending less than five years. They tend to be more educated and wealthier than members of traditional churches.

Yet although they are growing in numbers, almost one-third of the people attending megachurches give nothing financially, and almost half never volunteer. While there are many metrics by which we can evaluate the health of churches, it doesn't seem to be a good sign that these megachurches are struggling to connect their members with the practical work—giving, serving, transforming—that *every* church is *always* called to do in its local community.

One of the reasons for this may be the disconnection between the megachurch campuses and the surrounding neighborhoods—a dynamic similar to the isolation of suburbanites who live in gated communities. Most of these megachurches have created so-called third places *within* their buildings. Coffee shops, racquetball courts, gift shops, youth centers, outdoor patios, libraries, and comfortable lounge areas offer leisure and dialogue in comfortable and entertaining atmospheres—without ever needing to leave campus or interact with the surrounding communities.

This vision of "success"—comfort, expansive facilities, attractive surroundings—is sometimes the goal for traditional churches that are stagnant or declining. Since older church buildings rarely can create the atmosphere of one of these megachurches, the natural assumption is that the older church needs to grow, and grow quickly, so that it can afford to upgrade its facilities and attract more people.

Yet that begs the question: What *really* attracts people? Megachurches are attractive to potential members, but is that the only model of attraction? Does an older church need an extreme makeover to turn it into the latest and greatest church/restaurant/health club? Often these older, struggling churches can find informal places near their church buildings where they can connect with unchurched outsiders. Sunday school classes can relocate to coffeehouses or public spaces. Bible studies can meet in the local pub. Youth meetings can happen at the skatepark. As relationships are built outside the walls of their own buildings, these churches can gain fresh insights and creativity about potential space for the worshiping community—a process that makes the transition from mortar to mobile more purposeful.

The hazard of becoming attached to a particular church building isn't a new problem. One of Israel's biggest sins was its complicity with the pagan cultures that surrounded it. Israel repeatedly slipped into worship of fertility gods like Baal and other national religions, and they longed for a human king despite God's clarion call that he would watch over them as their ruler. These longings to be like its neighbors even influenced the way Israel thought about corporate worship. The tabernacle was a portable tent designed by God, so Israel, though a mobile people, could still enjoy a sacred place. As they moved through the wilderness after being delivered from slavery in Egypt, the Israelites would stop periodically for rest and worship. The tabernacle served God's sojourning followers well, and it was appropriate in function and its use of resources.

But once the Israelites became a settled people, the culture around them began to seduce their desires. They longed for a permanent temple that would testify to their power and splendor, so they cried out to King David for a temple in which to worship God. God eventually allowed David's son, King Solomon, to build the Jerusalem temple. That temple, which came to be known throughout the world, was a symbol of God's presence, and the inner sanctum, called the Holy of Holies, was the ultimate place of God's dwelling.

We in twenty-first-century America tend to place great importance on our own "inner sanctums," the physical sanctuaries where we come to meet and worship God each week. For sacred events like baptisms and weddings, it is hard for some of us to imagine any place other than our church building being appropriate. But we Christians *also* affirm the reality that God is everywhere. He is in our homes, our schools, and on our Little League fields; God is in our bars, our jails, and our sleazy hotels. God's Spirit is present in and penetrates all spaces of the earth and universe.

While we know this in principle, the practical implications of it seem too wide. How could we really meet God in those "unholy places," especially when the option of a safe, clean, and exclusive church building creates comfort and reverence? How can we leave the building and find our Lord's presence in the world? Can we really meet in a storefront or coffee shop, and really meet God in new and powerful ways?

These are questions the Israelites didn't grapple with often; once their temple was completed, it became their entire focus. We have reached a similar place with our massive number of church buildings—but is this the way it needs to remain?

God is still a "tabernacle God" who dwells where we are, especially when two or three of us gather. When that happens, even "secular" venues are "sacred" because God is there. As Christians, we must preach this *good news* to ourselves: God doesn't dwell in any one building!

The deep problems we sometimes experience by clinging to our buildings are more personal than theological. We simply *like* our buildings. They are where we've always been, and it's hard for us to imagine any alternative. Yet a robust "theology of place" reminds us that by our biblical calling, we are "pilgrims," not "settlers." When we lose our sojourner spirit in the communities into which God calls us, it becomes easier to focus on our own needs rather than on the needs of the communities God is asking us to transform.

Perhaps we can dare to turn our backs on our buildings and turn our faces to God. In the process, we can celebrate the freedom and new life that can come only when we let go of sanctuaries and begin to worship in tabernacles.

POWER

CHAPTER FIVE
POWER

I hope our wisdom will grow with our power,
and teach us, that the less we use our power the
greater it will be.
—Thomas Jefferson

Abused, Misunderstood—and Biblical

We often associate the word "power" with tyrants and dicta-
tors. Most of the time we view power negatively since so many
of us have had bad experiences with people abusing their power
over us, from bosses to spouses to church leaders to politicians.
Certainly the world is filled with controlling and manipulative
people who use power as a means to get their own way. Because
of these abuses and the tendency of Christians to emphasize
servanthood over authority, we can reach the natural assumption
that power is innately evil.

Nothing could be further from the truth.

Power is a major theme in the Scriptures, where it is used
for both good and ill. There are powerful armies, powerful

kings, powerful deeds, power encounters, and power that heals, reconciles, liberates, and forgives. Rome's power put Jesus on the cross, but his power conquered the last enemies, sin and death. There is power in strength and power in weakness. In fact, power is one of the constants from the garden of Eden in Genesis to the New Jerusalem in Revelation.

As congregations all across the country navigate the shifting currents of change, it is important that we understand power properly. Power can abuse; power can *empower* us to become who we were meant to be. And as we change to become agents of empowerment, we enable countless others in the body of Christ to become all God created them to be.

Conflict Multiplied by Personality and Personality Power

Change never happens in a vacuum. It always happens *to* people, *includes* people, and *affects* people. And wherever there are people, there are countless personalities and types of power that can come into potential conflict. Regardless of the practical and physical issues facing a church undergoing change—which alone are usually hard enough!—the process is almost always complicated by personalities and uses of power.

The Bible clearly acknowledges leadership as one of the gifts of the Spirit that edifies and builds up the church. Hundreds of books have been written on leadership and the innate and acquired components of healthy leaders. The Bible also speaks in 1 Timothy about certain qualifications a church leader, deacon, or elder should possess. An overseer should be a good family leader, well respected by those outside the church, self-controlled, hospitable, able to teach, not quarrelsome, and not a lover of money.

However, there are certainly other sorts of people who help to make an effective, healthy church body. One of the greatest challenges of any church—especially one experiencing membership decline, financial crisis, or other conflicts—is to have leaders who are directing the congregation in a way that values and utilizes the diverse personalities present. This is one example of a biblical use of power, for any exercise of leadership is an exercise of power. But what sort of power? The sort that seeks its own gain, or the sort that empowers every member of the church?

Perhaps it will be easiest to see what this sort of godly, biblical power looks like if we look first at other ways power is exercised. Wherever there are people—whether in the church or in the world—power is being used, either to the benefit or to the detriment of those people.

Political Power

Perhaps the most visible use of power in our country today is political power. Despite its ubiquity, few Americans are optimistic about the use of political power. There seems to be a growing backlash against the way that political power tends to be used for self-promotion and to assist special interest groups, rather than to improve the lives of common citizens. Political power is seen, often rightfully, as an insiders' game that has no time to help the powerless.

In contrast, the church, by biblical design, should be the least political group in the world when it comes to interpersonal relationships. As "brothers and sisters" reconciled by God and given different gifts to build each other up, there is no theological or practical room for Christians to abuse power—especially political power. We are to recognize each other as more important than ourselves, serving one another, bearing each other's burdens, and, most importantly, loving each other. This goes double for leaders in the church who, in opposition to their political counterparts, are called to lead lives of *less* privilege and to use power for others rather than for themselves. As a living organism, animated and led by Christ, we are to submit to *his* leadership and direction, which are the antithesis of any kind of human "special interests."

Yet because of our sinful nature, which tends to use power for selfish gain, churches can sometimes become as political as other systems that use control or influence to get their way. This political power may take the shape of an autocratic pastor or chairman of the board, an established Sunday school class that has used money and influence to sway opinion, or even from unsatisfied members who rally others to their cause. But whatever the opinion or cause, the bylaws of the church should not be the bottom line for decision making. Love is the final standard for the people of God, not getting one's way.

Yet a type of positive political power can have a place within the church. When Christians band together to fight injustice, even in their local neighborhood, they are using their sense of corporate call to stand against the evil and wrongs of their world. Others outside the church may likewise be invited to join efforts that are important. For example, community organizing can help build coalitions among schools, businesses, churches, and organizations to stand together against an issue seen as detrimental to the community. On a larger scale, there may be national or global issues that have veered from God's order or desires and that require wider political organizing. For example, unjust treatment of the mentally ill, children working long hours in sweatshops, human trafficking, and hunger issues—all are worthy reasons to use political influence to make changes. History has penned the tremendous impact of men and women like Mahatma Gandhi, Martin Luther King Jr., and Mother Teresa, who have influenced governments and policy to fall more in line with God's kingdom. Refusing to take up arms amid persecution, they have marched peacefully, challenged injustice, and defended the poor and marginalized. In each case, it was more than the leadership of these individuals that made the difference, because it took thousands of supporters to stand with them against injustices.

Financial Power

It should be no surprise that money plays a significant role in the change process of the church in America, the wealthiest nation in the world. We sometimes treat our money as if it were sacred—and even if we don't, we use its power to achieve ends that are less than God desires. Most congregations know that there are certain donors who use financial gifts to get their way. And when churches experience crises, money is almost always involved. If certain people who have been blessed financially threaten to leave the church or withhold their tithes and offerings, things get complicated quickly. On a smaller scale, though equally important, if a church member does not like the focus of the present missions program, he or she may give money to another missions agency instead. This story is repeated countless times each week—about carpet color, or staff choices, or church programs—and in each instance, the power of money is being used for personal gain, rather than for the kingdom of God.

Since so many churches in need of change are struggling with inadequate finances to pay the pastoral staff, keep the utilities turned on, and make the critical building repairs, finances will almost always be a point of discussion and disagreement. In so many ways, how members spend their own money is a statement of their practical theology. For example, if funds are insufficient, what gets cut? Does the pastor go? Do building repairs trump the missionaries the church has supported? Do programs get trimmed? All of these difficult choices exacerbate the growing tensions and quickly become the focus of disagreement, even when larger issues are obvious—and obviously more important.

Pouring money down an endless hole seems foolish, but the alternative of reimagining church is a greater challenge for many members. If struggling churches have the courage to face the underlying problems that have precipitated the abuse of financial power, they have hope of surviving. Money alone cannot transform a church that has lost its way—and money may, in fact, simply add weight to a church that is already drowning.

Relational Power

While political and financial power stare us in the face every day, there is another, more subtle power that is equally present. We can see it in the life of Jesus, an itinerant preacher from a backwater territory who nevertheless changed the world. He didn't have political power or financial power, yet he possessed more power than anyone in history. As his followers, we are called to exercise the same sort of power he did and thereby to be one of the greatest forces in the world.

How can this happen? The power of God's people is about relationships. Jesus asked twelve ordinary men to follow him, as well as dozens of other men and women over the course of his ministry—people in whom he saw potential. He knew their flaws, got frustrated by their personalities, and challenged them on their lack of faith. It was in that intimate, relational community that Jesus stretched them, encouraged them, and admonished them. Through acts of healing, words of truth, and constant examples of sacrifice and servanthood, Jesus empowered his fellow sojourners to continue his work after he was crucified. His work was transforming people and communities, and he knew the only way this would happen was through the growing power of relationships.

Perhaps the greatest sin of today's church is the lack of intimate relationships among church members. While many sanctuaries are filled to the brim with worshipers, there is often an infinitesimal number who share close relationships. In a busy world, there just never seems to be enough time after work, school, and family to talk about important things and serve others alongside each other. In a consumer-oriented culture, churches are chosen to meet our needs, not to be another organization that demands more time and energy.

Yet the power of relationships is exactly what allows churches to survive nearly any trial or change. Congregations driven by relationships can weather any struggle as their love for each other and for God brings unity and purpose. True relationships become the foundation on which to build difficult decisions about change. And it is that same ability to build and sustain relationships that provides relational churches with the power to change the world. Relational people have the skills to move past cultural barriers to work with those who do not share their values or beliefs. They can love immoral neighbors, cross racial and economic barriers, and find ways to serve those from other religions. They can even live out the call of Jesus to love their enemies and do good to those who hurt them.

Political configurations shift and change, and money ebbs and flows, but the power of true relationships is both deep and lasting, and that is the sort of power God desires us to acquire.

The Power from on High

At the Mount of Olives after the resurrection, Jesus met his disciples for the last time before ascending to the Father. Although he had taught them and modeled life for them each day for three years, his last commandment may have seemed a little surprising. "Do not leave Jerusalem, but wait for the gift my Father promised," he said. "You will receive power when the Holy Spirit comes on you; and you will be my witnesses in Jerusalem, and in all Judea and Samaria, and to the ends of the earth" (Acts 1:4, 7). Didn't they have power already? Was this something different?

It was. The coming of the God's Spirit at Pentecost empowered the new believers and birthed the church. From the first day of the fledgling new fellowship, those outside the faith did not understand it or what was happening. Probably confused and afraid of what they had seen and heard, they laughed and ridiculed those empowered ones as being drunk. Peter assured them that the controlling influence that had intoxicated them was not wine, but God's Spirit.

God's power established and grew the church. And without God's power today the church cannot change and will be trapped in its traditions and sinfulness. Only when we understand the difference between the dominating power of control and the enabling power of God's Spirit is there any hope of transformation.

The exercise of human power—political, financial, and so on—may "get things done," but it can never replace the work of the Spirit to empower followers of Jesus. Charismatic leaders can motivate and inspire members to feel excited about serving others, but only the power of the Spirit can send them out with God's compassion.

One of the greatest needs in the church today is not a new mission statement but the fresh wind of Christ's Spirit, which transforms hearts and minds. For a variety of reasons, many churches have not experienced the movement of God in their worship, Bible studies, or prayer meetings in years. That empowerment from the God who is a sender will naturally lead to a fresh vision of the church's purpose from their local neighborhood to the ends of the earth. It is the nature of God to send because he longs for the unbelieving and misdirected world to know his love. Yet countless Christians remain pew bound because they lack the Spirit's power to do ministry and to do even "greater things" than Jesus. Traditional churches from the West have been seduced to believe that good doctrine dictates worship and purpose, and that emphasis has eroded their sense of passion and call. Even postmodern Christians and house churches in North America struggle to reach out beyond their own confines and membership.

Even while the church in America and the West is shrinking, according to *Operation World*, the church throughout the rest of the world is exploding. In Africa, Christianity has become the religion of almost half of the population, with more than half a billion believers. Large-scale growth has occurred in places like Ethiopia, Sudan, and Benin. In Nigeria, all-night prayer meetings called "Holy Ghost Services" can average 500,000 in attendance.

Of all the continents, Asia has the most intense and widespread persecution and by far the most significant challenge to world evangelization, but Christian growth remains prominent. China alone has more than 100 million Christians. In South Korea, there are now as many as 50,000 Protestant churches, many of which meet to pray before work or at night and have watched the Lord of the harvest draw new believers into their churches. They have sent over 20,000 workers out to other nations to share the good news that Christ is Lord. Even believers from Muslim backgrounds in Asia are growing in numbers throughout the Arabian Peninsula and places like Iran and Iraq. In India, Christian growth is occurring predominantly among the tribal groups, Dalits, and lower castes of Hinduism.

Latin America has experienced unprecedented church growth. Much of that growth has come through Pentecostal and charismatic missionaries who understand the need for reliance on the Holy Spirit. Persecuted Christians from India to Iran have relentlessly faced harm without fear because of their dependency on the Holy Spirit. House churches in China, Nepal, and São Paulo have exploded in numbers through cell groups that believe both inward and outward journeys could and should coexist.

Even with unprecedented Christian growth, there are still 2.84 billion people considered unreached, 41 percent of humanity. To put it another way, over 40 percent of the world's people are counted among the least reached or unreached category and have no known Christians among them.

Amid the growth, various social challenges exist that the worldwide church must address. Poverty, human trafficking, civil war, HIV/AIDS, and other issues need the assistance of the church, and sometimes the specific help of the Western church. Yet the world is teaching the mission of God to the West. The

Spirit has already come, and he desperately desires to draw the body of Christ into the presence and power of God in worship and purpose. The call of the prophet Isaiah models the integration of the two. In the midst of the holy presence of God, he is broken by his own sin and unworthiness, only to experience deep forgiveness. God asks, "Whom shall I send? And who will go for us?" Having experienced the power and transformative work of God, without hesitation Isaiah proclaims, "Here am I. Send me!" (Isaiah 6:8). We are called to go out into the world in the power of the Holy Spirit and to experience forgiveness and grace in our worship—and Christians around the world are showing us how.

The Individual World Changer versus the Spirit-Led Disciple

We've seen how political and financial power are no match for the relational, Spirit-led power of God, whether experienced in individual hearts, church communities, or movements of renewal and mission that explode across the world. The power of God is without limit, and God longs for his mission of love to be accomplished in the heart of every one of his children.

Sometimes, however, it is all too easy for us to slip back into bad habits—to ignore the power and leading of the Spirit and instead take the responsibility upon our own shoulders. We think the world can be changed, and we're just the ones to do it!

Recently, at his request, I met a pastor new to the area for lunch in a local café. He knew of our urban ministry and wanted us to partner with him in the adjacent community. He was quite friendly and engaging as he began to tell me about his vision for his church to impact its community. It was an older, established church that was now down to only fifty members from its peak of well over seven hundred in years past. With an old building that had become too expensive to maintain and a graying group of five leaders who had weathered the catastrophic changes to this point, it was time to either close its doors or find a way to bring it back to life.

The new pastor was convinced he could do it! With a "take the bull by the horns" philosophy, in only a few months he had pushed the despondent leaders to the edge with his plans for change, including removing them from leadership to become a pastor-led church "for a season." But it was too much change, too fast, and with an untested new pastor. The few remaining members weren't going for it. As we ate lunch that day, I began to lose my appetite as I listened to him describe his recent "victories" to wrestle the leadership away from these five men in order to give him freedom to implement his new vision. With a lot of "God-talk," he justified every tactic and saw only the glorious future ahead. His pitch to garner our help to do community ministries was part of that plan. By the end of lunch, I was hedging every way I could. Something just was not right. There was an obvious lack of love and a defensiveness of his positions that sent my discernment meter off the charts. He was clearly using power selfishly, even though he justified it for God's sake.

And as one can see only in retrospect, three months later, it was all over and my gut feeling was confirmed. He'd had a significant moral failing that was broadcast across the local media. The church had fired him just before closing its doors for good.

There are times in our own personal self-deceit that power becomes manipulative and twisted. Without genuine relationships with godly peers who can confirm and support our intentions, we are often lost in the cause without the Spirit's power.

No amount of unloving and indiscriminate power can ever achieve God's purposes.

Whenever we think it's about *us*, it isn't. God doesn't ask us to accomplish his mission by being extra-super-effective ministers or missionaries on our own. It isn't about imposing our will on the world—it's about God's will transforming us and God's Spirit leading us into authentic renewal and mission in every corner of the world.

One of the greatest myths about change is that church leaders are more spiritually mature—a myth made clear by my story about the young pastor out to change the world. If we stop to think about it, we realize that having a leadership title or role doesn't automatically make one Spirit led. Those who are truly renewed and empowered for mission may have no formal leadership roles at all, yet it is to them that churches in the midst of change must listen. These Christ-centered members are most able to envision and introduce change and to love those church members who struggle with change in the process. Their dependency on God's urging for the church is balanced with their love for all the members, and they reject political and financial power in favor of the relational power of God's Spirit.

The spiritually mature—the spiritually empowered—know that change never depends solely on beliefs. While beliefs are a critical component of change, they are only a part of renewal and missions. To successfully navigate the process of change, real leaders recognize that the gifted change agents in the congregation might not be the existing leaders or the most vocal members. Instead, lasting change happens when God empowers his people for his mission in hearts, communities, and the world. That change is never accomplished with our own power, but, just as we see in the life of Jesus, with the power of godly relationships and a daily reliance on the Spirit.

PAIN

CHAPTER SIX

PAIN

Given the choice between pain and nothing, I
would choose pain.
—William Faulkner

In the last few weeks, two friends, both pastors of growing
churches, were fired. For the most part, neither saw it coming.
Both had been called to local churches with at least three hundred members who wanted to change: to move beyond being
only traditional to becoming churches of renewal and missional
practice. Both men had been very clear about their intentions
to transition the church from a program-based model to a
model that emphasized spiritual formation, the priesthood of
the believer, attention to the local community, and intentional
diversity. Both had created vibrant small groups where honesty
and accountability were encouraged, and more members were
getting out of the pews and into the world. There seemed to be
a general contentment in both congregations, and the elders of
both churches had recently approved the pastoral leadership in
annual evaluations.

Then, surprisingly, both men were asked to leave. Searching for answers in the midst of confusion, both men heard similar responses from the elder boards: *While we appreciate* some *of the good things you did, we wanted more organization and pastoring than you provided.*

Did these two churches approve of how their pastors were leading them through the process of change? Or did they disapprove? The answer is both! The transition from an attractional, internally focused church to a missional church is more difficult than most churches and leaders recognize, and churches can simultaneously support change and believe that it is simply too much to ask. There is still a common expectation that the pastor is the leader hired to orchestrate the dispensing of religious goods and services each week, and any interruption of this program is viewed as a failure. As Brad Brisco says, "The gravitational pull for us to focus all of our resources on ourselves is very strong" *(Missional Church Network).* We want our leaders to help us change while *simultaneously keeping things the way they've always been.*

It's no wonder that one of the key words for church change is *pain.*

No Pain, No Change

Unlike traditional church training that asks members to accept certain cognitive information, real change often comes at points of personal angst or conflict. In the pain we can choose to grow. When my wife and I traveled the world in 1984, we worked among the poor and oppressed in various countries. That brought us face to face—painfully!—with our own hypocrisy and wealth-based values. Having walked through slums of only a few of the world's 1.4 billion absolute poor, a deep sense of responsibility followed. From the pain of those encounters came the chance to accept responsibility and grow in the way we lived, prayed, and loved.

Since then, our ministry has been offering a poverty simulation weekend experience for students and adults. Though it pales in comparison to the realities and pain of those who are constantly hungry and poor, as participants feel the pain of several days' worth of poverty, they become significantly more teachable. When we allow pain to speak to us, and when we pause long enough in the change process to admit our feelings and gather our insights, the change produced is lasting.

This is a lesson that we can apply to churches that are changing. Pain is necessary—and it isn't as if churches are pain-free to begin with! "Churches simply cannot make significant changes and keep all their people pleased. Not everyone is pleased now" (Smith and Emerson, *Passing the Plate,* 189). Denial, avoidance, and blame only ignore the realities and delay the process. Moving beyond pseudocommunity—where being nice and getting along are often called "church"—we need new levels of inclusivity, commitment, and honesty. In other words, we need to admit the pain and then take the responsibility to deal with it. Along the way there will be fighting, pouting, resistance, passive aggression, and lots of blame to go around.

But if the church is to survive, we will have to learn to "fight gracefully," recognizing that real community requires integrity and that lasting change is always accompanied by pain.

Denial

Of course, accepting pain isn't the only option. We can simply pretend that the pain doesn't exist!

In his bestseller *Who Moved My Cheese?* Spencer Johnson creates an allegory of how different people respond to change. One of the characters simply refuses to believe his daily cheese is gone and, staring at the empty spot, becomes immobilized. Clearly one way that churches deal with the pain of change is to deny that anything is really happening.

Many of us believe that if only things stay the same, we can continue to be comfortable. And if things aren't staying the same? Well, then we can pretend like they are. After all, in a busy world, who has time to deal with all the challenges at the church? It seems hard enough to get our own houses and offices in order. The garage needs cleaning, the kids want a weekend campout, that new diet might be just the thing, and of course the bills have to be paid. With all this going on, the thought of tackling the bigger issues behind the church's diminishing attendance and unmet budget seems impossible.

So in the midst of our frenetic lives, the problems of the church simply do not make our list of things to do. Sure, they may be chatted about in Sunday school classes and after-church fellowships, but the leaders of the congregation know that to really face the challenges will mean a plethora of meetings, arguments, and hurt feelings, and there is the presupposed reality that little is likely to change anyway. Denial seems the easiest solution. Until things get worse. And they will.

Usually spawned by another broken air-conditioning unit or a lack of leaders for vacation Bible school, the congregation is forced to face the facts. And since continued denial and avoidance get harder and harder as signs of the church's poor health become more obvious, we do what is natural: avoid church entirely. We find ways to not be around, thus avoiding the guilt and frustration of a dying church. Our reasons sound legitimate, at least at first. "Got to see the parents this weekend!" "We're headed to a conference." "The kids have been sick." And as the reasons to be absent multiply, the congregation slips closer to the point of no return.

Soon death is inevitable. Willful ignorance, procrastination, and busyness speed what denial has already begun. Godly church change involves pain, and attempting to deny and avoid pain only produces another kind of change: church death.

It's Your Fault!

When denial and avoidance are no longer options, we still have a fallback plan: blame. Pointing fingers is as old as Adam . . . and Eve, Cain, Jonah, and almost every other Bible character we meet. Instead of taking responsibility for our actions, we point our fingers at others as a handy way out. The pastor and staff of a church in transition are easy targets. "If the preacher had better sermons, more folks would attend." "If everybody gave more, we wouldn't have these financial problems." "That youth director spends too much time playing with those kids instead of teaching them the Bible."

Yet, like the self-destructiveness of denial and avoidance, blaming others only compounds the problem. Blame is highly destructive in groups that are trying to move into true community and grow. Shannon Peck writes that condemnation, accusation, blame, criticism, and disrespect are toxic. "They cut deep," she says, and church bodies have a difficult time healing—and this at the very moment of change when health needs to be a priority (Shannon Peck, *Love Heals*, 218).

Blame doesn't need to be the final word, however. When Christ followers care enough about his church to see things as they really are and take personal responsibility for some of the sickness in our local churches, we have a real chance to accomplish lasting, Spirit-led change and emerge as a living, growing force for renewal and missions in our communities and in the world. This means listening, studying, praying, risking, giving, and changing, as well as giving time to the process that could have been spent in personal recreation. And this means pain, as change always does.

But we have not been given a spirit of timidity, but a spirit of power. And if our churches fail to change, it will be *our* fault.

Getting Personal

In the late seventies, after years of joy in the traditional church, I began to struggle. I came to think that the early church, described in Acts 2:42–47, had been most true to what God wanted for his church. It seemed to capture the essence of the body of Christ with daily contact, shared meals and possessions, and learning from the apostles about the things Jesus did and said. Convicted that Christianity was best lived out through incarnational living among the poor, my wife and I bought a house in the middle of a blighted African American neighborhood, which had once been a wealthy area until the "white flight" to the suburbs in the sixties. Having purchased a huge, 4,000-square-foot house for only $12,000, we moved in with our family to a rat-and-roach hotel, formerly occupied by two mentally ill veterans, a nineteen-year-old construction worker, and the "Cat Lady," who collected forty felines in her nightly runs in the alley trash bins. After gallons of pesticide and long days of renovation, the old house was at least livable. Even in the midst of nightly gunshots, fights outside the bar across the street, and prostitutes working our street, we began to feel at home.

In the months and years that followed, we welcomed college students who wanted a more "radical" and community-based lifestyle. After work or school, we would invite low-income children and teens to the house for backyard Bible clubs and recreation on our newly poured concrete basketball court on the adjacent lot. Through the years, other Christians moved nearby to join our high-stakes call to the inner city. We worked on each other's houses, babysat for each other, ate many meals together, and enjoyed some of the best conversations about faith and discipleship we had ever experienced.

Since virtually all of us were disenchanted with our churches, we decided to meet together for worship on Sundays. Without tradition determining our worship style and teaching, we enjoyed the creativity of various members. One week we would have teaching, followed by dialogue and Communion. Another week might include acting out a parable, including several of the children. One woman brought candles; another brought a challenging tape to listen to; still another brought a map to show the locations of unreached peoples and persecuted Christians. We always ate together and agreed where to send our weekly offerings. Gradually, a few of the neighbors began to attend. Most everyone felt a sense of love and "body life" of which they had never been a part. This was church!

Yet within three years, our little neighborhood church fell apart. While we continued to grow, some of us focused on deepening relationships with each other, while others felt like we were ignoring our call to minister in the neighborhood. My wife and I were in this second group. With full-time jobs, family, and so much time committed to "church life," we had little left over to serve others, yet that was what we longed to do. So after much conversation, we determined to leave with the church's blessings. The others hung on about nine months longer until the whole church ceased to meet, and some held significant resentment toward others as they separated. The church we thought would someday be an example to all other Christians was no more.

As our little church imploded, I found myself numb, detached, and hopeless. If this church, with all its good intentions, effort, personalities, theological background, and location could not work, maybe no church could. With three young children, two of whom were old enough to sadly miss their "church friends," we felt compelled after a few weeks to find another place for them to attend Sunday school while we licked our wounds and decided what to do next. Over the next few months, we attended a large church with a pastor who seemed to genuinely care about our pain and the grief we were experiencing and had no problem with us just attending while we healed. Through those months, we tried not to focus on what went wrong and who was at fault, but clearly those questions recycled through our brains and emotions almost daily. In time, the hurt and sadness lessened and seemed to pop up only on occasion.

Through the pain of that church experience, God eventually brought healing. In the following years, we experienced a deeper humility than ever before. Abiding in Christ became more important than starting something new. That submission to God seemed to be the foundation through which he chose to eventually call us to the poor and marginalized and use our own gifts in ways we never imagined. We would never have asked for the pain, but in time God clearly used it for his own glory.

Little Ventured, Little Gained

It is hard to move toward newness and change without openly acknowledging the pain from losing what was once meaningful, healthy, and life giving. Particularly when a difficult circumstance or crisis causes a church to enter the change process, there is usually a temptation by high-control leaders to push the process forward before others in the congregation have had time to mourn the loss. When a church chooses to transform itself, or even when a pastor dies or runs off with the secretary, there is sadness and grief and even anger. Attempting to fix the problems without some kind of corporate mourning will likely delay the grieving process and can frequently sabotage the renewal process. Because grieving is personal and complex, no one can create a timeline or know when it will end. Commonly acknowledged stages of grief are described as numbness followed by strong feelings from nostalgia to anger, then drifting, and finally recovery. Depression or emptiness, as deep as they are, can become cathartic in spiritual renewal. We all experience death and loss. It is basic to our humanity. But for many folks, especially in an individualistic society, corporate bereavement may be harder to share. In the midst of the healing process, some church members may lash out at others or cast blame as an inappropriate expression of their own unresolved hurt and pain.

"Blessed are those who mourn, for they will be comforted" (Matthew 5:4). In the Sermon on the Mount, Jesus embraces open grieving as part of the healing process. In our pain-avoiding culture, which tends to push feelings to the side in an effort to get back to work, we need to hear his words. It is only after our weeping and sorrow that our "grief will turn to joy" (John 16:20).

Churches that have become self-centered and inward must come to a place of confession and mourning for their corporate sinfulness. They will come to embrace the self-emptying act of Jesus, the Suffering Servant, in his darkest hour that preceded the greatest hope ever known. There is "death to self" in the renewal process—our own dark hour, when we seem to finally come to terms with our finitude and pain, and we trust that only the living God can bring the healing and rebirth needed for personal renewal. The miraculous power of a church's corporate "death" to its own aspirations and selfishness is soil from which real change grows.

PITFALLS

CHAPTER SEVEN
PITFALLS

There is no way to take the danger out of
human relationships.
—Barbara Grizzuti Harrison

Some of our best friends struggle with substance abuse. One of the most painful things is to hear that one of our friends in recovery has relapsed. After months or sometimes years of being clean and sober, one weak moment can propel that person back into dependency and shame.

Men and women who choose to start afresh in their recovery often talk about the "triggers" that led to their relapse. For some it was extra money, a separation or divorce, or the invitation back to the "bright lights" of a party or sports event. It could also be physical tiredness, spiritual emptiness, or emotional confusion. While the triggers vary with each individual, most all of us can relate to the "stinking thinking" that lures and tempts us back into patterns of behavior that we know are destructive.

This is more than a personal issue. The reality is that we bring our triggers into community gatherings and corporate conflicts—and if our church is undergoing change and transformation, we may find ourselves behaving in ways we thought we'd recovered from. That's why it's so important to know what our change-triggers are, so that we can avoid the pitfalls that doom so many local congregations before change has even begun.

Trigger One: Giving Up

Maybe it's not worth it. Let's just give up.

This pitfall may snare more than any other. Before change has even truly begun, we've already given up and let despair set in. And let's be honest—when a church is undergoing change, there may be many legitimate reasons for such despair! As we saw in chapters two and six, local congregations may become more discouraged as they recognize their deficits and acknowledge unhealthy realities previously unseen or ignored.

However, when we admit defeat without seriously acknowledging the transformative power of God's Spirit, we are revealing our low view of the church. Biblically understood, the church is a living organism, capable of growth, change, renewal, and overcoming outside threats. If it is true that "the gates of Hades will not overcome" the church (Matthew 16:18), giving in to despair before there is more clarity about what God is doing or can do is faithlessness.

If despair is a trigger that kills church change, hope—or at least patience—makes it possible for a struggling church to change into something different, and better, than its current expression or model. It might be led to join collectively with another congregation, bringing new hope and direction to both groups. It may decide to become a cell-based church and only meet in large groups occasionally. The possibilities of what God can do with a teachable, hopeful congregation are limitless. God is the change agent, not us. It is the power of the transforming gospel that makes all things new, and healthy churches learn to recognize and reject despair.

James said it best: "Let perseverance finish its work so that you may be mature and complete, not lacking anything . . . Blessed is the one who perseveres under trial because, having stood the test, that person will receive the crown of life that the Lord has promised to those who love him" (James 1:4, 12). The Christian who is discouraged can find deep comfort that God's work is being done in the midst of the struggle. The apostle Paul knew how important perseverance was to growth in faith as he challenged the Ephesians. These painful struggles, both in the world and in the church, become the opportunities to grow in faith, "until we all reach unity in the faith and in the knowledge of the Son of God and become mature, attaining to the whole measure of the fullness of Christ" (Ephesians 4:13). Several years later, the apostle John, writing to the seven churches in the book of Revelation, complimented the church in Ephesus, "You have persevered and have endured hardships for my name, and have not grown weary" (Revelation 2:3).

What a compliment it is to churches today that "continue to continue" in the midst of hardships, rejecting despair and choosing to hope.

Trigger Two: Doing the Same Thing and Expecting Different Results

Albert Einstein is attributed by some for the famous saying "Insanity is doing the same thing over and over and expecting different results." Our friends in Alcoholics Anonymous frequently repeat this phrase since they recognize their own destructive tendency to return to the same habits and patterns that caused their addiction in the first place.

Churches that have been doing the same things for years must realize that the culture *has* changed, even if the church has not, and many people have become disenchanted with the same old church programs, Sunday school, revivals, pipe organs, and Wednesday night prayer meetings. No matter how we try to dress these habits up with a few cosmetic changes, or paint the sanctuary and hang up some hip new banners, we will fail to reach a growing segment of the population.

It's never easy to consider changes to programs that were deeply meaningful to the older church members, yet we must do so for the sake of the younger generation. For example, weekly "life groups" that meet in homes are supplementing or replacing Sunday school in many changing churches. Unlike the more formal Bible study times before the worship service, the home groups enjoy gathering informally in the comfort of a living room, where it is natural to share a meal, share personal needs, and discuss a portion of Scripture. Once Christians experience the warmth of these small groups, they are less likely to get their children awakened early and dressed in "church clothes" to go to a Sunday school class. Yet for some more institutional churches, changing the Sunday school hour seems like abandoning the church, even as attendance at the traditional hour continues to diminish.

Recovering addicts know that there is a long and difficult adjustment to changing behaviors. While some addicts talk boldly of how they are going to change their lives, statistically most of them fall back into their substance abuse when they "go it alone." But when they go through treatment, they learn new thinking and behavioral changes that slowly begin to replace old habits. However, even then, it is challenging not to go back to the comfort of old patterns, such as dysfunctional family relationships, Friday night gatherings with old friends, and extra money on paydays, which quickly break down logical thinking with the assumption that "this time will be different."

Like those overcoming addiction, churches must also admit powerlessness in our lives and faith in a "Power greater than ourselves to restore us to sanity." The millions of recovering addicts recognize that a "searching and fearless inventory of our lives" is necessary for changes in behavior that lead to real freedom. Change is difficult, and it is always easier to keep doing what we've always done. Yet if the results are destructive and not producing growth in quality and quantity, it is insane to continue the same programs and practices and expect different results.

Trigger Three: Trendiness

In our 24/7 culture of instant change, it can be hard to know what is merely fashionable and what is truly appropriate. Churches are never immune. Whether new "branding" schemes on the signage, electronic debit card machines in the pews, youth meeting rooms filled with arcade games, or coffee shops in the foyer, it is often difficult to discern which of these is the next "hot" item and which is genuinely a cultural adaptation that congregations appreciate. To a growing postmodern culture, "church clothes" are forever out for Sunday worship, replaced by jeans and shorts. Pipe organs and hymnbooks make no sense to a generation raised on iPods and YouTube.

Unfortunately, in a Christianized culture of consumerism, a growing number of church consultants is feeding on dying congregations. With graphs and charts that sell a struggling congregation on their "proven" success that guarantees a turnaround church, they offer package deals that can be very attractive. Especially in the midst of church leadership dysfunction, the ears of frustrated members can really perk up with these stories of "success" among churches that were going down for the count only to rise up and win the fight. While few of these for-profit consultants have ill intentions, many rely more on cultural trendiness than Spirit-led ecclesiology—after all, how can you condense the movement of God's Spirit to a few PowerPoint slides?

It may be true that with cosmetic changes, congregations may grow, at least for a while. Yet once a church commits to luring outsiders to attend based on the latest fad, the essence and identity of that church are diminished. Religious consumers are no different from mall shoppers, and they'll move on to the next church when a better deal is offered. That's why the trigger of trendiness must be identified and avoided, and why God's good news is always culturally relevant.

Trigger Four: Grasping

I get amused at all the infomercials that promote yet another exercise contraption or weight-loss program. Presented by good-looking, well-shaped, and enthusiastic professionals, they are masterful at selling the public their "can't fail" device with "scientific proof" and testimonies from successful clients. Some of the weight-loss products look so ridiculous that it is easy to laugh and wonder who would really buy this product.

But people do. That's why the commercials continue: because they work. When someone is overweight and out of shape, he or she is always vulnerable to a quick fix. The sad news is that just a few weeks after the "wonderful deal if you call in the next ten minutes," the miracle machine is jammed next to several other such devices in the garage. There just aren't any quick fixes for weight loss—at least not until the next infomercial!

When churches become desperate to fix their decreasing membership and dying church, there are some leaders and members who move into infomercial mode. "I heard about a church where the pastor shaved his head if 75 percent of the Sunday school class attended on one Sunday morning, and they did!" Suggestions seem to come from everywhere and everyone. "We could do this or that, but we must do something," they say. From selling the parsonage to firing the pastor, and from buying a church-growth DVD series to advertising a sermon series about sex, the prevailing attitude is that if the church can just buy or do the right thing, right now, everything will change.

It is in these quick-fix times that the church needs to rediscover the peace of Christ that brings real focus on who *we* are and who *God* is. Only when a struggling church clings like a branch to the vine does it bear fruit. "I am the vine; you are the branches. If you remain in me and I in you, you will bear much fruit; apart from me you can do nothing" (John 15:5).

Notice that the verse doesn't say "apart from me and the latest church-growth conference."

Trigger Five: Ignorance

American humorist Josh Billings once said, "The trouble ain't that people are ignorant; it's that they know so much that ain't so." So it could be said of many of us! Ignorance should never be glossed over, even if it is said with passion and conviction. Yet we are so willing to speak so profoundly about that which we really do not know. From old wives' tales to the latest Internet rumor, there is plenty of ignorance to go around, and plenty of us are happy to repeat it.

The Bible recognizes that foolishness abounds all around us. "Fools find no pleasure in understanding but delight in airing their own opinions" (Proverbs 18:2). It seems that when things get tough, foolish words multiply! There will be those in a struggling congregation who will speak foolishly about things they don't understand. While open meetings in church do have their place so that all can be heard, a church-wide meeting that spews untruths and ignorance can do more harm than good. Good leaders realize that facts and realities can create a foundation for discussion and exploration that will be healthy. That process may begin with a call to prayer and fasting and a reminder to seek God first for true wisdom and understanding. "If any of you lacks wisdom, you should ask God, who gives generously to all without finding fault, and it will be given to you" (James 1:5). It is critical to build God's house on the rock instead of the shifting sands of opinions based on empty thought. Proverbs remind us, "Though it cost all you have, get understanding" (Proverbs 4:7).

As the process of church change moves into honest discussions of the issues and choices for the congregation, a discernment process, likely led by those leaders in the church who are acknowledged to have gifts of wisdom and understanding, can prevent random opinions from sabotaging the church.

Trigger Six: Divisiveness

Infighting has existed since the church began. Sinful humans can always find something to disagree with each other about, and that disagreement can easily get nasty. When we stake out territory in a doctrinal or social battle, we stop listening. The result is usually hurt feelings, gridlock, and damaged relationships.

A struggling church that needs to change is vulnerable to divisiveness. Uncertainty can bring out the worst in congregations. Paul wrote to the church in Corinth about this situation. "You are still worldly. For since there is jealousy and quarreling among you, are you not worldly? Are you not acting like mere humans? For when one says, 'I follow Paul,' and another, 'I follow Apollos,' are you not mere human beings?" (1 Corinthians 3:3–4). He appealed to them in Christ's name to "agree with one another in what you say and that there may be no divisions among you, but that you be perfectly united in mind and thought" (1 Corinthians 1:10). This strong-willed church planter did not mean that opinions were wrong or that conflict was to be avoided. His very style included confrontation, yet Paul clearly believed that loving God meant loving those with whom we disagree. He would not accept most church divisiveness, and neither should we.

In his prayer for the disciples and all believers, Jesus asks the Father that his followers be unified, even as the Father and Son are one. Interestingly, the impact of this unity is "so that the world may believe that you have sent me" (John 17:21). Regardless of how disappointing it is to see a church die, it is worse for a congregation to self-destruct in anger and infighting, which impacts the unchurched world's ability to believe that Christ is real. Unity is a sign of maturity, even in the midst of strife. "Make every effort to keep the unity of the Spirit through the bond of peace" (Ephesians 4:3), and "Whatever happens, conduct yourselves in a manner worthy of the gospel of Christ" (Philippians 1:27).

Trigger Seven: Too Little, Too Late

Most patients warned by their doctors of impending health problems do little to change their condition until it is too late. Changing behavioral patterns—eating better, exercising, and so on—is difficult. Often it takes a crisis, and not simply a warning about a crisis, to get us to act.

Churches experiencing life-threatening symptoms tend to follow the same pattern. While the signs of sickness are all around, congregations fall into the pitfall of doing too little, too late. Either they make minimal changes that won't really transform their health, or they continue to ignore the problem. While many church members may talk in the foyer about their concerns and fears for the church's future, life goes on week in and week out with few serious attempts to honestly assess the needs and address them until it is too late.

Inaction is often worse than action. Being overweight, eating poorly, and lack of exercise may not affect an individual for a while—yet the longer healthy habits are ignored, the more likely that health complications will eventually surface. If no legitimate process is being implemented to explore change, even a small group of church leaders or members may need to speak up and fervently request action. These pleas do not have to be posed as ultimatums or demands. But with genuine love for the bride of Christ, church members can encourage their leaders and fellow members to "wake up" and examine congregational health. It is best if such requests can be done collectively, instead of individually, to avoid the leadership dismissing the issue. Since time is important in this fragile stage, a definite process with timelines might be requested, especially since delayed responses are common when painful issues are at hand.

Since the unity of the faith is critical, these efforts to move toward action should be done with humility and pure motives so that they are not seen as threatening power grabs. And if we notice such efforts in our own congregations, our goal is then to "spur one another on toward love and good deeds" (Hebrews 10:24) as we begin the process of change.

Know Thyself

Do these change-triggers ring true in the life of your church? Do you see yourself on one side or the other of these hot-button issues? Before pointing fingers, perhaps some personal reflection about your own change-triggers would be helpful.

Which two of these pitfalls above are you most likely to fall into, and why? They aren't flattering, so be sure you are in a place where you can be completely honest.

___ Giving up

___ Doing the same things over and over and expecting a different result

___ Desiring trendiness more than deep change

___ Grasping at any solution that might work

___ Being ignorant of the real issues and possibilities for change

___ Causing divisiveness to protect yourself

___ Waiting too long to deal with a problem

We humans are such a confusing mixture of good and evil. Capable of incredible acts of compassion and mercy to help the poor and needy, we are also capable of hurting others deeply, even those we love. The Bible is a powerful narrative of the inconsistencies of God's people. From being a man after God's own heart to an adulterer and a murderer, King David was only one of a succession of God's servants who fell from their own sin. Yet even Rahab, a prostitute, found favor from God and made the list of the faithful in Hebrews 11. Since Scripture reminds us in Jeremiah 17 that our hearts are deceitfully wicked, it is extremely important that we admit and know our own sinful nature. Bringing hope and change to the church does not mean we are spotless and pure, but it *does* mean we can, in humility, be used by God in significant ways and for his glory.

Being aware of our own pitfalls, and even sharing those tendencies with others in the church, is a prerequisite to being an agent of change. In fact, it is that very admission of our failings that makes God's grace in the struggle so amazing. As we seek his kingdom in his Spirit, we find small victories in controlling our temper, being silent at the right time, praying instead of cursing, and building up those whom we might have formerly resented. The God-given paradox of it all is that sometimes it takes stressful church dilemmas for us to confront our weakness and sin—and then to walk forward together as the body of Christ through the power of Christ.

POSSIBILITIES

CHAPTER EIGHT
POSSIBILITIES

God has put within our lives meanings and
possibilities that quite outrun the limits
of mortality.
—Harry Emerson Fosdick

Dreams of What Could Be

Churches, like individuals, often become so stuck in the
quagmire of life's challenges that dreams seem like a luxury, more
like distant wishes than real possibilities. For many congregations, it has been too long since their leaders and membership
sat together and dreamed, imagining what it would look like if
their congregation broke free and became the church God wants
them to be. Declining or stagnant membership, tight budgets,
an aging population, internal focus on programs and services,
and decaying buildings can kill dreams before they begin to
grow. The result is congregations that live and breathe hopelessness, assuming that God's dreams of change and transformation
are meant for others.

But such dreaming is critical for the life and hope of the church. Once a body of believers thinks its mountain of problems is too high to climb, it will never see the summit of God's glorious opportunities. One of the most motivating components of hope is to discover "turnaround churches" that have overcome their near-death experience and watched God bring new life and purpose to them. They are emerging all over our nation.

Not Ready for the Cemetery Next Door

Twenty-one miles outside the small, rural community of Dublin, Texas, sits a century-old church adjoining a cemetery. Dublin has a population of only 3,779 folks and is only known as the home of the oldest Dr Pepper bottling plant in the world. Cottonwood Baptist Church is even more remote, sitting in the midst of farms and ranches "and the smell of cow manure," says its website. The building is unimpressive, and the parking lot looks like a pasture. Little hope would be available from church renewal manuals or from church consultants, who would not give this church any hope of survival, much less making a difference in the world.

There are dying churches next door to the dead in rural communities like this all over America—but this church isn't dying! If fact, it is very much alive. In 1985, while attending seminary, Mike Fritscher accepted the pastorate of the tiny congregation of thirty attending members, only as a stop on his way back to the big city when he completed his degree. Never in his mind did he imagine what God had in store for him and this dying church.

As God began to break Mike's dreams for a "successful" future with a growing call to bring God glory through Cottonwood, things began to change. They began to meet, pray, and dream about what God could do if they followed him in the rural countryside. Not everyone agreed about the direction, but a corporate spirit of listening to God and each other dominated those meetings. The little church began to grow in numbers and love for each other. Thirteen years later, the congregation had grown to 150 members who gathered to pray and consider God's growing call to the nations. "How could a small rural church really make a difference in the world?" they wondered.

Yet as they listened to God's missional call in those days of prayer, they committed to follow wherever he led. It didn't take long. Within the month, a team from the church went to central Asia and sensed God's leadership to begin church planting among an unreached people group. Today there is an indigenous church of over a hundred new believers there because of Cottonwood Baptist Church's faithfulness.

Being sensitive to God's Spirit was just the beginning this journey of sending; the months and years ahead were filled with opportunities for the church. God opened new doors at every turn, from their own small community to the ends of the earth. They have been involved in work in Turkey, Mexico, Africa, and among Navajo Indians in Arizona. At home, they offer ESL classes for Spanish speakers and Celebrate Recovery for local folks struggling with addiction. Cottonwood has a ministry called "Kids Across Culture," which brings clean water, health care, and educational opportunities to the global poor. They have sent out over a hundred of their own members to serve in places around the world. "Missions is not something we do; it is who we are!" says Pastor Mike. "We are invited to participate with God in what he is doing and bring glory to him! It has not always been easy, but we have learned to listen and be faithful."

The results are amazing. Today there are nine hundred worshipers attending the church each Sunday in this town of less than four thousand! Members of all ages are remarkably diverse considering the local demographics. Scores of new, formerly unchurched Christians fill the pews. There is an excitement in the air as they meet, knowing that God is still moving and renewing them. He has created "new wineskins" to hold the expanding vision of the church, including new leadership structures, worship, and training to fit their missional call to love each other and serve the nations.

While the tombstones at the cemetery next door still remind each Sunday worshiper at Cottonwood that life is temporal, the members have seen God make alive the dry bones of a dying church that many doubted could ever live again. God has breathed new life into the deadness. "I will put my Spirit in you and you will live" (Ezekiel 37:14).

So it is with the church today. Whether from impending problems or just wanting to be more genuine, congregations stand at a crossroads and have to make decisions about how God is calling them. The conclusions should not be made based on survival or safety instincts or from the expectations of others, but on the call of the Holy Spirit to be the hands and feet of Jesus in the city in which he placed them.

Gotta Have Faith

It's tempting to think that our circumstances prevent us from dreaming big dreams. We assume that if things were a bit easier—if we had more time, more money, more energy—we'd start dreaming again about what might be possible.

However, the real issue is not our circumstances, but our lack of confidence that God is already working in and through those circumstances and that he can empower us to live into our dreams at any point in life. "Now faith is confidence in what we hope for and assurance about what we do not see. This is what the ancients were commended for" (Hebrews 11:1–2). Noah, Abraham, Isaac, Jacob, Joseph, Moses, David, the prophets, and others were people "who through faith conquered kingdoms, administered justice, and gained what was promised" (Hebrews 11:33). We've seen that successful change isn't about a formulaic program, but about faithfully following God's call. "Without faith it is impossible to please God" (Hebrews 11:6), and God will reward his people who sincerely seek him. Even mustard-seed-sized faith can get us through the crisis as we sink into the waters of despair as Peter did before Jesus reached out to save him (Matthew 14:31).

Once a struggling congregation can begin to faithfully dream God's dreams, it will join the ranks of the persecuted and martyred whose faith in the midst of crisis helped bring God's kingdom. While this suffering "cloud of witnesses" may not seem like a group we want to hang out with, they are the heroes of our faith who show us that *it can be done*. Guaranteed "results" and "success" are not part of the deal with God, but the walk of faith always unites us with the One who loves us perfectly and has already prepared good things for us to do in his world.

There are few biblical examples of faith more powerful than the story of the three Jewish men, Shadrach, Meshach and Abednego, who refused to lose hope even in the midst of what would have been a painful death. Ordered by King Nebuchadnezzar to worship his golden idol and serve his gods, they stood firm, saying, "We do not need to defend ourselves before you in this matter. If we are thrown into the blazing furnace, the God we serve is able to deliver us from it, and he will deliver us from Your Majesty's hand. But even if he does not, we want you to know, Your Majesty, that we will not serve your gods or worship the image of gold you have set up" (Daniel 3:16–18). These young followers of God were grounded in the truth, believing that uncompromising obedience to the living God, even if it cost them their lives, was worth the price. They understood that their role was only to be faithful and obedient—and to let God do the rest.

The journey will be hard. Besides personal and corporate renewal of church members, it will likely involve structural and theological adjustments for your church. Certainly it will require significant missional changes that will affect how members spend both their time and their money. There simply are no road maps on this journey or "five easy steps" to a new church life. The flames *will* get hot and require a new level of faith to see what is not yet present. As Paul wrote to the church in Philippi, "He who began a good work in you will carry it on to completion" (Philippians 1:6). Faith is built on God and his purposes, not on our abilities, what others have done, or even brilliant ideas. All hope for the church must be grounded in Christ, who gave himself for the church. Praise be to God that we are not responsible for saving ourselves!

On Your Mark. Get Set. Go!

We've been on a long journey together and covered a lot of information. Principles, anecdotes, questions, verses, stories—all of these have helped us understand the nature of church change. We've looked at why we need it, how to prepare for it, what to do in the midst of it, and how to avoid the pitfalls that accompany it.

The most important thing we've learned, however, is that change begins and ends with God, not us, and it is only through God's power and love and grace that any change can last. No matter what happens to your church, Christ has not given up on you, your church, or the church universal. He is Lord. Begin and end there. Cynicism, blame, and despair are not biblical options. Take heart, have faith, and don't give up on the potential and possibilities of your church transforming.

Many years ago, my wife and I were privileged to meet Mother Teresa in Calcutta, India. For one week we traveled by rickshaw to the "Mother House," where the Sisters of Charity, the Catholic order that Mother Teresa directed, took care of men and women in their final days and hours of life. Each day we went to area train stations to find dying beggars and carry them back to the Mother House. In the next few hours, nurses and volunteers would bathe them, bandage their sores, shave them, and offers bites of food and sips of water to those who could still manage to swallow.

What we learned above all from the Sisters of Charity was that, more than the critical efforts of healing, the most powerful medicines were the acts of hands-on compassion. Some sang to the patients as they helped, some smiled during the most unsavory tasks, and others had broken conversations. In every action, the focus was on dignity. The love of the sisters for God compelled them to extend that radical love to the destitute and dying, giving them an unimaginably precious gift: the chance to change from outcast to friend, from untouchable scum to dignified human, even in death.

We learned these things in Calcutta, but it wasn't until much later that we understood these lessons weren't just about human bodies, but about the body of Christ, the church. Some churches are outcasts, too, ready to die and unloved by anyone except the members.

The paradox of the local church and the universal church is this: churches may die—may even *need* to die—but the church will never die.

If a church in need of change determines that a gentle goodbye is more Christlike than a bitter fight or hurt feelings among members who have come to love each other through the years, then so be it. The church is temporary. The kingdom of God is eternal. The church can even look for creative ways to give away its brick and mortar and various possessions that will bring honor to God. How much better is this than hoarding it all until it is too late to work together for a peaceable and generous end?

God is the perfect giver, and even in death his gifts are manifold.

Back in Hometown, USA

Let's go back to the park we visited in chapter two. What if you could invite Jerry, Frieda, and the rest to your house for a meal and a conversation? After all you've read and learned, how would you encourage them to see God's greater purposes at work in the American church? How would you respond to the limited and insufficient viewpoints of civil religion, traditionalism, postmodernity, and noncommittal wandering? How would you continue the conversation into the weeks and months following, ensuring that every personality called by God remains part of his church and part of his transforming work in hearts and in the world?

Your response to this diverse group of friends gets to the core of your critical role in church change. The church is made up of people like you—ordinary Christians who are tired, busy, and uncertain about what exactly they have to offer. Such Christians can be tempted to leave things the way they are rather than undertake the arduous process of change. Yet we've seen that change isn't optional—it's God's essential way of making sure that his people remain faithful and missional in a world crying out for the good news. If you can understand where Jerry, Frieda, and the rest are coming from—and where they might need to go—you are already equipped to be the change agent your church needs.

Through change, God desires to bring healing and hope to the body of Christ where you worship. God's Spirit will give you new energy, fresh insights, and sufficient grace as you depend on him in prayer. God will surprise you with a ray of hope when things look the darkest, and he will send you friends for the journey who will remain faithful through it all.

Inside your church are real people—like Ray and Curtis and Norm—who can be saved from their own negative experiences, apathy, and hopelessness. Even now they are waiting for an invitation to have coffee, for a real word of honesty in the parking lot after the service, or for a bag of groceries to get them through the month.

In other words, they're waiting for change. Will you help them?

In the apostle John's final revelation, there are seven symbolic churches, each of which is affirmed or admonished. We recognize that in the midst of God's desire and expectations for his church we remain messy sinners who never seem to get it quite right. God sees our deadness, our complicity, our lack of repentance, and our false prophets—and God also sees our perseverance, our selflessness, and our deeds.

Through all of this, God continues to love the church—so much so that he allowed his only Son to die and be raised again. It is now the calling of the body of Christ—my calling and your calling—to live generously and fearlessly in a world that desperately needs to see Jesus high and lifted up. Our task is noble, and in all honesty we will fail many times. Only through God's Spirit can we become, again and again and again, God's agents of change and transformation.

The church is God's plan for the world. To believe anything less is to deny God himself. So let us hold to the hope that God isn't finished with us yet. There remains work to be done, and we are the ones being called to do it.

DOES YOUR CHURCH NEED TO CHANGE?

APPENDIX

DOES YOUR CHURCH NEED TO CHANGE?

The following questionnaire can help your church understand where it is in the process of change. It can help sensitize a congregation to components that affect its "body life." It may be most helpful to ask each individual in the church to complete these sixteen questions without any discussion or clarification. (Feel free to make copies of these questions for them.) Then create several groups of three to five people to try to synthesize their answers into one document for each group, knowing there will be some disagreement about finding a single answer. Before the church's first "health checkup," which may initiate a journey of conversations, have a small team summarize the various groups' answers into a single document. This compilation is not to be further discussed but simply used as a barometer of the potential change process. The lower the score, the higher the probability of successful change. And while higher scores may indicate potential danger for church life, they don't mean that longevity or stability are bad in themselves. They should be seen only as warning signs to go slowly and carefully through the chapters in this book, which deal with the issues that often sabotage success.

Rate your congregation's present change factors:

1. Most members are between the ages:
- (1) __ 14–29
- (2) __ 30–39
- (3) __ 40–59 ✓
- (4) __ 60 and older

2. Number of years in same location:
- (1) __ 0–5 yrs.
- (2) __ 6–14 yrs.
- (3) __ 15–25 yrs.
- (4) __ 26 or more yrs. ✓

3. Approximate age of worship center:
- (1) __ 0–5 yrs.
- (2) __ 6–10 yrs.
- (3) __ 11–19 yrs.
- (4) __ 20–40 yrs.
- (5) __ 41 or more yrs. ✓

4. General attitude and attachment to current building and/or site:
- (1) __ Believe it's time to move
- (2) __ Recognize a need to consider other locations/options
- (3) __ Prefer to stay if at all possible
- (4) __ Refuse to move

5. Number of years the senior pastor has served your church:

(1) __ 0–5 yrs.

(2) __ 6–10 yrs.

(3) __ 11–19 yrs.

(4) __ 20–30 yrs.

(5) __ 31 or more yrs.

6. Demographic/population of church building area (economic and/or racial):

(1) __ Few changes in area

(2) __ Beginning to see changes

(3) __ Significant changes occurring

(4) __ Major changes occurring

7. Demographic of congregation attending Sunday services:

(1) __ No single majority race or class

(2) __ Other races/classes total 33% or more of population

(3) __ Other races/classes total 21–32% of population

(4) __ Other races/classes total 10–20% of population

(5) __ None or few from other races/classes (0–9% of population)

8. Financial condition of church:

(1) __ Strong and stable

(2) __ Lowered budget last year

(3) __ More budget cuts coming

(4) __ Financial crisis imminent

9. Worship style:

(1) __ Contemporary & Traditional

(2) __ Liturgical

(3) __ Contemporary

(4) __ Traditional

10. General attitudes toward future:

(1) __ Mostly optimistic with vision

(2) __ Mostly ready for change but not sure how

(3) __ Mostly confused and uncertain

(4) __ Mostly negative or hopeless

11. General attitudes among members:

(1) __ Encouraging and supportive of each other's ideas

(2) __ Genuine effort to listen to each other

(3) __ Some negativity and complacency

(4) __ Lots of conflict and disagreement

12. Leadership style of those currently in charge:

(1) __ Interested and affirming of various ideas of members

(2) __ Genuine effort to listen to members

(3) __ Creates discussion opportunities but needs control or last word

(4) __ Dominating or apathetic

13. Spiritual condition of church:

(1) __ Deeply prayerful and led by the Spirit

(2) __ Majority are spiritually mature

(3) __ Relatively immature spiritually

(4) __ Members tend to be more legalistic or self-centered

14. Objective evaluation of the church:

(1) __ In last five years, a consultant or committee has guided a process of examination of most aspects of church life

(2) __ Occasional examination of some components of church life in last five years

(3) __ Casual evaluation of a few areas of church in last ten years

(4) __ No evaluation done of life and ministries of church in last ten years

15. Change precedence:

(1) __ In last three years, church has dealt positively with a major change in the church (e.g., new pastor, significant member growth, started a mission church or new ministry, church-changing revival or renewal, built new building, etc.)

(2) __ In last three to five years, church has experienced a few major changes that have been mostly positive

(3) __ In last five years, church has had a significant loss that members still grieve (e.g., key members moved, pastor left, major budget cut, etc.)

(4) __ In last three years, church has experienced a split or major crisis that has a continued negative impact on the church

16. Missional exposure and training:

(1) __ There are frequent sermons and training around being a missional (holistic) church

(2) __ Somewhat regular theme in sermons and some training to impact community/world

(3) __ Occasional sermons and little training to be a more missional church

(4) __ Almost no preaching or training about holistic, missional view of the purpose of the church

---

Total points from above: *How healthy and ready for change is your church?*

Your Score: _____

Score Grid: *(the lower the score, the more capacity for change)*

16–27 Healthy and capable of change

28–39 With some work, change can occur with minimum negative impact

40–52 Change process will likely be messy and painful

53–64 Likely that change process will be destructive

BIBLIOGRAPHY

BIBLIOGRAPHY

American Piety in the 21st Century: New Insights to the Depth and Complexity of Religion in the US. Waco, TX: Baylor Institute for Studies of Religion Research, Baylor University, September 2006.

Arbuckle, Gerald A. *Grieving for Change: A Spirituality for Refounding Gospel Communities.* London: Cassell Publishers Limited, 1991.

Bandy, Thomas G. *95 Questions to Shape the Future of Your Church: Tools to Fulfill the Congregation's Mission.* Nashville: Abingdon Press, 2009.

Barna, George. *Leaders on Leadership: Wisdom, Advice and Encouragement on Leading God's People.* Ventura, CA: Regal Books, 1998.

Barna, George. *Revolution: Finding Vibrant Faith beyond the Walls of the Sanctuary.* Ventura, CA: Barna Books, 2005.

Barrett, David, et al. *World Christian Encyclopedia: A Comparative Survey of Churches and Religions—AD 30 to 2200.* New York: Oxford University Press, 2001.

Barrick, Audrey. "Study Compares Christian and Non-Christian Lifestyles." *Christian Today*, February 7, 2007, http://www.christiantoday.com/article/american.study.reveals.indulgent.lifestyle.christians.no.different/9439.htm.

Bonhoeffer, Dietrich. A letter to his brother Karl-Friedrick, Jan 14, 1935.

Bosch, David J. *Transforming Mission: Paradigm Shifts in Theology of Mission.* Maryknoll, NY: Orbis Books, 1991.

Brisco, Brad. "Transitioning from Traditional to Missional." Missional Church Network (blog), May 20, 2010, http://missionalchurchnetwork.com.

Burke, Daniel. "Big Churches Posting Small Membership Losses." The Pew Forum on Religion and Public Life, March 2, 2009, http://pewforum.org/Religion-News/Big-churches-posting-small-membership-losses.aspx.

Claiborne, Shane. *The Irresistible Revolution: Living as an Ordinary Radical.* Grand Rapids: Zondervan, 2006.

Clowney, Edmund P. *The Church: Contours of Christian Theology.* Downers Grove, IL: InterVarsity Press, 1995.

Conder, Tim. *The Church in Transition: The Journey of Existing Churches into the Emerging Culture.* Grand Rapids: Zondervan, 2006.

Dally, John Addison. *Choosing the Kingdom: Missional Preaching for the Household of God.* Herndon, VA: The Alban Institute, 2008.

DeVries, Dave. "Missional Transformation: Fueling Missionary Movements that Transform America." Doctoral diss., Bakke Graduate University, 2007.

Deymaz, Mark, and Harry Li. *Ethnic Blends: Mixing Diversity into Your Local Church.* Grand Rapids: Zondervan, 2010.

Dorrell, Jimmy. *Trolls and Truth: 14 Realities about Today's Church That We Don't Want to See.* Birmingham, AL: New Hope Publishers, 2006.

Dorrell, Jimmy, and Janet Dorrell. *Plunge2Poverty: An Intensive Poverty Simulation Experience.* Birmingham, AL: New Hope Publishers, 2006.

Emerson, Michael O., and Christian Smith. *Divided by Faith: Evangelical Religion and the Problem of Race in America.* New York: Oxford University Press, 2001.

Everist, Norma Cook, ed. *The Difficult but Indispensable Church.* Minneapolis: Fortress Press, 2002.

Ewert, Alan W. *Outdoor Adventure Pursuits: Foundations, Models and Theories.* Scottsdale, AZ: Publishing Horizons, 1989.

Guder, Darrell L. *The Continuing Conversion of the Church*. Grand Rapids: Wm. B. Eerdmans Publishing Co., 2000.

Halter, Hugh and Matt Smay. *And: The Gathered and Scattered Church*. Grand Rapids: Zondervan, 2010.

Hart, Dirk J. "Insights into Congregational Growth." Faith Communities Today, 2007, http://faithcommunitiestoday.org/sites/all/themes/factzen4/files/FACT_Cong_Growth.pdf.

Hartford Institute for Religion Studies. "Fast Facts about American Religion," http://hirr.hartsem.edu/research/fastfacts/fast_facts.html.

Herrington, Jim, Mike Bonem, and James H. Furr. *Leading Congregational Change: A Practical Guide for the Transformational Journey*. San Francisco: Jossey-Bass, 2000.

Hirsch, Alan, and Debra Hirsch. *Untamed: Reactivating a Missional Form of Discipleship*. Grand Rapids: Baker Books, 2010.

Johnson, Spencer. *Who Moved My Cheese? An Amazing Way to Deal with Change in Your Work and Life*. New York: G. P. Putnam's Sons, 1998.

Kinnaman, David and Gabe Lyons. *Unchristian: What a New Generation Really Thinks about Christianity . . . and Why It Matters*. Grand Rapids: Baker Books, 2007.

Kolb, David. *Experiential Learning: Experience as the Source of Learning and Development*. Upper Saddle River, NJ: Prentice Hall, 1984.

Linthicum, Robert C. *Building a People of Power: Equipping Churches to Transform Their Communities*. Colorado Springs: Authentic, 2006.

Mandryk, Jason. *Operation World*. Colorado Springs: Biblica, 2010.

Mann, Alice. *Can Our Church Live? Redeveloping Congregations in Decline*. Herndon, VA: The Alban Institute, 2000.

McLaren, Brian D. *A New Kind of Christian: A Tale of Two Friends on a Spiritual Journey*. San Francisco: Jossey-Bass, 2001.

McLaren, Brian D. *Everything Must Change: Jesus, Global Crises and a Revolution of Hope*. Nashville: Thomas Nelson, 2007.

McNeal, Reggie. *The Present Future: Six Tough Questions for the Church.* San Francisco: Jossey-Bass, 2003.

Mezirow, Jack. *Transformative Dimensions of Adult Learning.* San Francisco: Jossey-Bass, 1991.

Minatrea, Milfred. *Shaped by God's Heart.* San Francisco: Jossey-Bass, 2004.

Missional Church Network, http://missionalchurchnetwork.com/what-is-missional.

Missional Network: Missional Church Archives, http://www.missionalnetworkweb.com. North American Mission Board.

Nessan, Craig L. *Beyond Maintenance to Mission: A Theology of the Congregation.* Minneapolis: Fortress Press, 2010.

New Monasticism, http://www.newmonasticism.org/12marks.php.

Newbigin, Lesslie. *The Open Secret.* Grand Rapids: Wm. B. Eerdmans Publishing Co., 1978.

O'Connor, Elizabeth. *Journey Inward, Journey Outward.* New York: HarperCollins, 1975.

Oldenburg, Ray, ed. *Celebrating the Third Place: Inspiring Stories about the "Great Good Places" at the Heart of Our Communities.* Cambridge, MA: Da Capo Press, 2002.

Peck, M. Scott. *The Different Drum: Community Making and Peace.* New York: Simon & Schuster, 1987.

Peck, Shannon. *Love Heals: How to Heal Everything with Love.* Solana Beach, CA: Lifepath Publishing, 2003.

ReligiousTolerance.org, http://www.religioustolerance.org/chr_prac2.htm.

Reveal, http://www.revealnow.com, spiritual online survey for churches.

Robinson, Anthony B. *Transforming Congregational Culture.* Grand Rapids: Wm. B. Eerdmans Publishing Co., 2003.

Roxburgh, Alan J. *Missional Map Making: Skills for Leading in Times of Transition.* San Francisco: Jossey-Bass, 2010.

Roxburgh, Alan J., and M. Scott Boren. *Introducing the Missional Church: What It Is, Why It Matters, How to Become One.* Grand Rapids: Baker Books, 2009.

Rusaw, Rick, and Eric Swanson. *The Externally Focused Church*. Loveland, CO: Group, 2004.

Samuel, Vinay, and Chris Sugden, eds. *Mission as Transformation*. Oxford: Regnum Books, 1999.

Satterlee, Craig A. *When God Speaks through Change: Preaching in Times of Congregational Transition*. Herndon, VA: The Alban Institute, 2005.

Schockley, Gary, and Kim Schockley. *Imagining Church: Seeing Hope in a World of Change*. Herndon, VA: The Alban Institute, 2009.

Schoel, Jim, Dick Prouty, and Paul Radcliffe. *Islands of Healing: A Guide to Adventure Based Counseling*. Hamilton, MA: Project Adventure, Inc., 1988.

Seibert, Jimmy. *The Church Can Change the World: Living from the Inside Out*. Waco, TX: Antioch Community Church, 2008.

Shelley, Marshall, ed. *Empowering Your Church through Creativity and Change: 20 Strategies to Transform Your Ministry*. Nashville: Moorings, 1995.

Sider, Ronald J. *Just Generosity: A New Vision for Overcoming Poverty in America*. Grand Rapids: Baker Books, 2007.

Smith, Christian, and Michael O. Emerson. *Passing the Plate: Why American Christians Don't Give Away More Money*. New York: Oxford University Press, 2008.

Snyder, Howard A. "The Energies of Church Renewal." *Journal of Theology*, United Theological Seminary, 1989.

Snyder, Howard A. *The Problem with Wineskins: Church Structure in a Technological Age*. Downers Grove, IL: InterVarsity Press, 1975.

Stark, Rodney. *What Americans Really Believe*. Waco, TX: Baylor University Press, 2008.

Stetzer, Ed. *Planting Missional Churches: Planting a Church That's Biblically Sound and Reaching People in Culture*. Nashville: B&H Publishing Group, 2006.

Stetzer, Ed, and Warren Bird. *Viral Churches: Helping Church Planters Become Movement Makers*. San Francisco: Jossey-Bass, 2010.

Stetzer, Ed, and Thom S. Rainer. *Transformational Church: Creating a New Scorecard for Congregations.* Nashville: B&H Publishing Group, 2010.

Swanson, Eric, and Rick Rusaw. *The Externally Focused Quest: Becoming the Best Church for the Community.* San Francisco: Jossey-Bass, 2010.

Thumma, Scott, and Warren Bird. "Not Who You Thought They Are: A Profile of the People Who Attend Megachurches." Harford Institute for Religion Research, June 2009. http://hirr.hartsem.edu/megachurch/megachurch_attender_report.htm.

Van Gelder, Craig. *The Missional Church in Context: Helping Congregations Develop Contextual Ministry.* Wm. B. Eerdmans Publishing Co., 2007.

Viola, Frank, and George Barna. *Pagan Christianity: Exploring the Roots of Our Church Practices.* Wheaton, IL: Tyndale: 2008.

Warren, Rick. *The Purpose-Driven Life: What on Earth Am I Here For?* Grand Rapids: Zondervan, 2002.